SURVIVING YOUR LIFE

WRITTEN BY A SELF-DIAGNOSED GLUTEN
INTOLERANT, SOCIALLY/GENERALLY ANXIOUS,
CLINICALLY DEPRESSED, HIGHLY SENSITIVE,
EXTROVERTED INTROVERT WITH SOME OCD
INCLUDING DERMATOPHAGIA? AND
INTERMITTENT EXPLOSIVE DISORDER.

Published by T.J. Sparks

© 2020

For H.N.B.

For never once raising an eyebrow

Fragile! Please Handle With Care

Now before you go thinking this self-help writer is a neurotic paranoid 'labelling junkie' freak, *I need to add neurotic paranoid 'labelling junkie' freak to the front cover* I'm not actually a fan of labels. I just want to lighten the mood a little to take you on this journey of discovery with me. Because humour and playfulness are the basic, fundamental keys to being connected to ourselves, others and the universe. Do you remember when we were children and we found the silliest of things funny? And how we would just let that laughter out and not even think about sweeping the area first for other people's permission and guidance on if it was appropriate to do so. Or care about how daft we looked giggling and rolling around on the floor, holding our stomachs because they hurt so much from proper belly laughing. We believed in Father Christmas and the Tooth fairy. We had invisible friends. We believed there were monsters under our beds at night and hidden worlds with unicorns and dragons at the back of our wardrobes. We actually believed in magic! Think about that for a moment. Your happiest carefree times were when you believed in magic. And we were not only allowed to believe in magic, we were actively encouraged to do so, and our imaginations could and did run wild and free like the untameable wind. We believed anything was possible because we never once thought about the downsides to anything. The logical part of analysing everything to death and spending most of our time in the future or the past was not something our brains had learned to do yet. We lived primarily in the present. Then one day out of the blue we had all of our magic bubbles cruelly burst, and we were told that we were no longer allowed to believe in these wondrous things, and that it was now time to get 'real' and to become part of the adult world, where logical and critical thinking rules.

We currently live in a time of 'extreme labelling'. We want to be known as being part of a group we feel related to in some way, or that gives us some feeling of identity or belonging, and less alone. We feel safe being part of a faction, much like we did hanging around in our little gangs at school. People will generally sum up another person in 2 minutes of meeting them. And they do this by labelling this other person, by pigeonholing them so they know who and what they are dealing with. We are doing this constantly every time that we come into contact with new people. Labels such as 'extrovert' 'geek' 'jobsworth' 'people pleasure' 'loser' 'narcissist' 'village idiot' 'princess' 'drama queen' can spring to our minds on these first encounters. We like to try to figure people out as quickly as possible, so we know where they fit into our lives. Whether they are someone we click with instantly and want to spend more time with, or that they are someone we are going to instantly cut off from getting to know us on a deeper level. Now in theory this method sounds pretty efficient, but the trouble is humans are so much more complex than a few sticky coloured labels. I tell people I'm an extroverted introvert because I know I am an introvert at heart, who loves nothing better than time to myself to read, write, watch movies and recharge my batteries in complete peace and calmness. But I also love to socialize sometimes and go to new places where there is a lot of noise with multiple energies buzzing around, and meet new people and generally 'have a laugh,' so makes sense I am this label right? But here's the thing, I have a couple of friends who also class themselves as extroverted introverts, and although there are undoubtedly similarities between us, there are also many differences. Which is where the danger comes from labelling ourselves and others too much, as it restricts us from growing, and shrinks our opinion of the world and the people in it.

We declare that we have all these food intolerances; Gluten intolerant, Lactose intolerant, Dairy intolerant, Caffeine intolerant. And although yes in lots of cases that will be true, in other cases people will wrongly diagnose themselves as they will see this as a fit for them. Also, it makes people lazy. A lot of the time we can sort our problems out, even food intolerances can be reversed with the right diet and detox program. Quite often food intolerances are caused by inflammation, which can most definitely be reversed. I'm not saying this is fact in every case, but surely it is worth a try, rather than saying to yourself 'well yep that's me, that's my label, so I don't need to do anything off my own back now to make the situation better. I will just sit back and let the experts of that particular label tell me what to do, how to act, what to eat, what to wear.' Labels are so final. They allow us to accept what we are told and to leave it there, instead of using our magnificent brains to think of new ways to understand and fix the problems of the world today and the humans in it. We want things to be simple, but by thinking like this we start making our magnificent brains simple.
Tell them you are part of the S.A.S.

I have suffered from crippling social anxiety most of my life. And although I can tick off most of the social anxiety sufferer (s.a.s) checklist, I don't comply completely. Because I lead what would be classed as a normal life to most people; I have always worked, I left home at 16 and supported myself financially ever since, I can drive and own a car, I have had long term relationships, and I can attend social functions not only without having a full scale panic attack but am also able to enjoy myself and 'appear' incredibly sociable. So, because of this I am told I am a 'highly functioning' social anxiety sufferer.

In my younger years I spent a lot of time on S.A. forums because I believed this was who I was. I had felt something was seriously wrong with me for quite some time, and I thought it was a malfunction in me alone, and that I just wasn't wired correctly. I worried constantly about the panicked thoughts and reactions I was having when I was around people which seemed to be getting worse. The constant blushing, the excessive sweating, the fear of talking in a group situation at work or socially, feeling like something really bad was about to happen ALL of the time. Then one day I stumbled across an article on social anxiety and it was a real 'eureka' moment. I could not believe it. It described all of my symptoms to a tee. I was no longer a circus freak. What I had wrong with me not only had a label, but other people had it too. I remember being so excited about the prospect of speaking to these 'others.' I'd finally be able to share these Martian-like feelings I had with someone. They would have similar stories to me. We could help each other. I would no longer be alone. So, I spoke to and met up with many fellow S.A. sufferers from the forums and attended social anxiety support groups. But I didn't meet someone I could share my feelings or stories with as I had hoped. I didn't actually meet one single person I felt I had 'anything' in common with, in fact it felt the exact opposite. I couldn't help but feel the ones I met or spoke with had a lot of 'other' problems and were very inwards and didn't want to open up and talk 'deep' with me. They also seemed to have accepted S.A. as their lifelong label and weren't really open to pushing themselves to find out why they had it, or to find a way out if it. Social anxiety was 'who they were.' The support groups were the worst part. They not only left me feeling disheartened because they weren't giving me the connection and recognition I needed, I came away feeling a fraud, because the clients and facilitators had trouble believing I actually had social anxiety because I came across confident and I had a life. So, I wasn't socially anxious 'enough' to be there it seemed. It left me feeling even more of an alien, why could I not just fit in somewhere? It was even more confusing for me because I knew how I felt inside, but everyone that knew me would never notice the S.A. They only ever saw me as a very warm engaging person with a charming positive nature??! Which is why labels are so ambiguous, as what we label ourselves is not the same label other people give us. Therefore, who is right? Us or them? And do we really need a get out of jail free card for every little obstacle we come across? Like did you know there's a label for being shit at maths? (well that's another one for me) It's known as a 'mathematics disorder.' And road rage? Yep, this is covered under 'intermittent explosive disorder.' *maybe I should have mentioned that to the security guy at the supermarket when I launched my trolley into that big stack of toilet rolls that one time. He might not have looked so terrified. It might have even made him laugh.* I have learnt over time that we are far better embracing the idea that we as humans are constantly evolving, changing and adapting to the new situations we find ourselves in. Therefore, if someone bites their nails (or the skin around them - dermatophagia) for 20 years, it doesn't necessarily mean they will do that for another 20 years. If someone has been depressed or anxious for most of their life does not mean that they can't one day become in control of their life, and not only decide they want to be 'truly' happy but they make it happen. First, we need to start questioning our labels. Then decide what we want to do with them, keep them or snip them off. There is a superb saying today 'before diagnosing yourself with depression or low self-esteem first make sure you are not, in fact, surrounded by arseholes.' Let's investigate these labels, then tackle them. For example, road/trolley rage is just an old program that humans have run for years and years. We usually first start watching the program in our parents, and then most other adults we've had the pleasure of being in a car with. And then we start running that same program in our systems when we grow older and start driving a car ourselves because it seems natural, and it's the only driving program we know. But once we are aware that is all it is as with most anger issues today, we can sack that program off, delete it and replace it with our own 'road resilient' program where we are completely in control of our emotions, and are calm and operating at our best.

Write down all the labels you can think of for yourself under 2 different headings

Labels I give myself

Labels other people give me

So, who is behind my labels?

Tara Jean

I knew from the age of 4 I was different from other people. I was unlike anyone I knew or had known up to that point, which consisted of my family, their friends and my school classmates. I can still to this day recall vivid recurring nightmares I had around this age. One was with a lion waiting for me at the top of the stairs in our house every night before I went to bed, and the fear I felt in my dream of having to try and get past without it mauling me to death was agonizing. Another was a giant spider bigger than me would appear at the door to the kitchen which I was already trapped in, so I would then have to try and edge past it, and it would usually electrocute me with one of its bright green glowing legs. And although these were extremely frightening, the dreams that truly terrified me were the ones where I was completely invisible to my mother, and I was trying desperately to get her attention and get her to see me. Sometimes in the dream I would be pulling at her apron. *Aprons, are they still a thing?* And she would be just carrying on as normal doing the dishes or ironing, completely oblivious to me crying and pleading 'mummy mummy.' Other times in the dreams we would be out walking, her in front, her pace too fast for me as I run to keep up with my little legs and I try to slip my hand into hers, but she snatches it away and puts her hands in her pockets and carries on at top speed as I get left behind on the street crying and begging again 'mummy mummy.'

I can understand now in my adult brain that I was already highly anxious at that age, and that instead of feeling loved, secure and protected, I felt overpowered, controlled and ignored by the people in my life.

There were 3 children: my brother, my sister and then me. We were brought up in North London by our parents in an extremely strict Irish catholic household with crucifixes above our beds, a holy water font by the front door, and scary religious lenticular pictures on the walls. One of them was of Jesus, which at first sight he was all happy and serene looking, but move your head to the side slightly and it would become a torturous Jesus, with blood pouring down his face from the painful crown of thorns digging into his head. *Jesus Christ, who makes this stuff?!* What I find funny looking back at this now is that our mother was so strict and controlling with what we were allowed to watch on television. She didn't want us to watch anything too adult or inappropriate such as horror films, but yet there I was living day to day in the house of horrors! I would spend hours as a child staring at the lenticular pictures, seeing how quickly I could get them to switch between the two versions, light and dark. And I had a lot of time to do this, as I was never allowed out to friend's houses or have them over at our house. I wasn't even allowed to go out to play with the children that lived on my street as my mother thought they were out of control heathen riff raff that would be a bad influence. I never really got on with my siblings growing up either, they always felt like strangers to me my entire childhood, and they thought I was weird and too quiet, and the only time they would interact with me was to be mean. My sister had it far easier than me as she was the same age as a girl who lived on the next street who had ancient parents that my mother liked very much, so she was allowed to spend a lot of time over there, and I can't blame her that she preferred it there to our house, so I hardly ever saw her. My brother spent most of his time shut in his bedroom, which I didn't mind at all. I did like my father though. I could sometimes feel his sensitive nature when I was sat with him. But unfortunately, he worked 2 jobs, so those moments were rare. I got used to the feeling of being alone most of the time and unsurprisingly went into myself. I found solitude in reading books and writing amusing little fantasy stories where I could instantly transport myself to a magical world where I had a new family who were colourfully wonderful. Needless to say, I was quite enthusiastic about starting primary school when I was 4, where I would finally get to play with other children and be somewhere that wasn't home or church. The trouble was by the time I got to school I had already been reading children's books for quite a while, and the classes there usually consisted of a lot of language learning using flash cards with words such as 'dog' 'cat' 'him' and 'her.' I was instantly problematic for the teacher as I already knew all that stuff and then some. So she would let me play in the big Wendy house in the corner of the classroom while the others learnt their words. I didn't mind, in fact I loved it. I was used to spending a large amount of time on my own already, and I loved the Wendy house. I can still picture it as clear as day now, it had pink walls, delicate little white chairs, a kitchen with a red plastic cooker with matching red plastic pots and pans, and a little window on the side with red and white gingham curtains. I would spend hours playing in there on my own. The teacher tried to get my parents to agree to put me up to the third year class as she felt I was too advanced for first year and wanted me to carry on learning at the level I was at rather than sit out, not be included and wait for everyone else to catch up. My mother wasn't keen on the idea as she thought it might disrupt me too much, she didn't want a fuss made, so I got to play in the Wendy house, a lot. School wasn't as I had hoped it would be. I had thought maybe I was just different from my family and that there were other people out there who would appreciate my weirdness, but in just the first few days of being there I was exposed publicly for being different and odd because I knew too much for my age. Instead of seeing myself more advanced than everyone else as a positive thing I made it a negative. A voice inside told me learning was 'bad' and that I'd never fit in being cleverer than everyone else. I spent the next 30 years trying to fit in.

My parents both came from dysfunctional family units in Ireland. My father was abandoned as a baby by his mother after she was abandoned by his father. She was only 16 when she got pregnant with him and was shamed into giving him up and was then banished to England by the rest of the family to keep the shame from their door. They didn't want to take responsibility for my father as they already had their hands full with their own kids, so he was put into care. My mother had what seemed like a normal family with 5 siblings and both parents, but her father was a very cruel and harsh man who would beat them and my grandma regularly. He treated them all with utter contempt. He was a firm believer that children should 'neither be seen, nor heard.' I am told this was fairly common for that time though. He then also abandoned them when my mother was around 9 and disappeared off to England, returning 10 years later to claim what was lawfully his; the house. Women didn't have a lot of rights back then and the man was more favoured. So, when he returned after many years away my grandmother had no choice but to let him stay. She hated his guts though and made it clear they were only married outside of the house, to keep shame from the front door. So, they made a deal that from then on that they would live together separately, pretending the other one didn't exist, and never speaking a word to one another. He lived in the back bedroom of the house with his own television in there, so he didn't need to sit in the lounge with her, and she slept in the front bedroom. This was where my family and I spent the whole 6 weeks of every single summer school holiday until I was 14.

My parents both moved to England separately when they were 18 to find work and a better life and met each other when they were 20 at a dance hall. Then you know the rest; marriage, shortly followed by 3 children. We were never a family that talked about anything 'ever.' I knew from a young age this 'felt' wrong, but I couldn't understand or talk about my feelings because I didn't really know what feelings were. My parents had repressed all of their own feelings from their childhood and were filled to the brim with stress and anger because of it. We were never given any affection physically or emotionally. We were smacked and whacked for stepping out of line and ridiculed for having independent opinions. But because we never went without anything such as food, clothing or toys I didn't see this as abuse. Shame was also a huge factor in my parent's life. It had been passed down from Christ knows how many generations and was their biggest driving force in whatever they did. If you went through something difficult or even traumatic, the shame of having the neighbours know and gossip about it was far more distressing than the trauma itself. Like my grandma who had to pretend to the neighbours that her husband hadn't left them without saying a word, but was really working in England and sending them money home regularly and that when he returned their marriage was still as strong as ever. The neighbour's opinion mattered more than your own family's opinion. In fact, most of my mother's conversations to us when we were growing up were about The Murrays who lived up the road from us at no.12. They represented what the perfect family was to my mother. 'I bet the Murrays wouldn't do that' was one of her favourite lines. 'I bet Mary Murray (the mother) doesn't have to put up with this' was another. Because of my mother's deep unhappiness in herself she could never see the positive in anything, including us. She could never be grateful for anything she had, including us. I remember her telling me once rather flippantly "you were a mistake you know? We only wanted 2 children, a boy and a girl so we didn't want another one." So yes, we were only ever told negative things growing up and nothing we did was ever good enough. If I did well at something there was always a critical comment about what I hadn't done right or well. The focus was **always** on the negative. In fact, I never even knew what praise was until I was an adult, and I cringed at the way it made me feel so much so that I would avoid getting it at all costs. And because we never received any approval at all when we were younger, all 3 of us stopped trying to get it and accepted we weren't worthy of it. We accepted The Murrays were better than us, which led to all 3 of us having profound low self-esteem as adults.

So, you see although I was somewhat aware of having anxiety as a young child, I was also aware I wasn't allowed to feel that way. I had to hide it away. As that certainly wouldn't have been good enough. And definitely something that would have shamed my parents to death. And I would have probably got a good hiding with the slipper too. *Is this why I can never wear slippers? Even the cute fluffy ones?*

Religion was another big negative influence in my life. I probably don't need to tell you about the control that can come with religion and how it can feed an already anxious self-judgemental mind. 'God is watching you all of the time to make sure you don't mess up.' 'If you don't follow the rules you will be turned away from Heaven and sent downstairs to burn for an eternity in Hell.' Having to go to Mass every week as a child and be brainwashed by the same repetitive ritualistic hypnotic procedure each time was pretty brain numbing and dumbing for me, when all I really wanted to do was play outside with the heathen kids in my street who would eye me up quizzically when we would walk past them in our fancy dresses and immaculate hair every Sunday morning. Those kids of course didn't go to my school, because catholic schools were few and far between, so my school was much further away.

Everything around me as a child growing up was fear driven. Home, school and church all conveyed the same messages and signals to my young fresh absorbent mind, that you must follow the rules and act the same as everyone else to be accepted, otherwise you will be punished and ostracized. We are told cults are evil and harmful. But if you look up the definition of a cult, it will tell you that first it has to have a leader or leaders, then there will be some form of indoctrination or education that seems to be coercive; usually brainwashing or mind control, and it will have some form of exploitation involved, and will usually use peer pressure to keep the members in line, it is completely fear driven. And that fear insidiously worked its way into my system as I had no proper defence against it, as I hadn't been shown another way of living. So, I did the only thing I could do, I shut down and went into myself completely. I even had to give up writing the fantasy stories and reading the delightful books because I no longer wanted to **feel** anything, including the joy they brought. I found unusual coping mechanisms to deal with blocking out the thoughts and feelings, I would talk to myself non-stop out loud to drown them out, and I started throwing a tennis ball up against the wall back and forth. I would do this for hours and hours at a time. I did this right up until I was 16.

And now for the interesting part about all of this!

My brother and sister lived in the exact same household as me, and had the exact same upbringing as me, but they didn't experience what I experienced!

I didn't find this out until much later in life, only a few years ago actually, from when I started on my healing journey and wanted to try and build a relationship with them both. Little did I realise that the conversation that followed from this would blow my world apart.

They both suffer with anxiety and different issues that have majorly held them back in life, which I am in no doubt is to do with our upbringing, but unbelievably they hardly remember our childhood and have no real feelings about it! They are what I refer to now as 'surface people'. You can never get too deep with them; they don't like it. I can only talk to my brother about travel or work, he will instantly change the subject or walk away if it's remotely probing. I've had more success with my sister. Actually, I've had some fascinating conversations with her in the last couple of years, because we never really spoke much to each other before that, and if we did it would only ever be surface stuff. But once I started on that journey 3 years ago, I knew I had to go back to the beginning. So, I took a bottle of wine in one hand and a spiritual spade in the other to my sister's house to see what I could dig up. 'The conversation' I refer to went like this:

Me: "Hey, do you remember the weird thing with our grandad?" (The one that lived in the back room of my grandma's house)

My sister: looks at me like I've just shown her my green alien blood, then finally catches up to real time and says: "weird in what way?"

Me: thinking ok where do I go with this now? So, I say "well he lived in that back room, didn't he? And well, we weren't allowed to talk to him, were we?"

My sister: Frowns, then looks puzzled, then her eyes dart frantically around the room, then finally centres herself and calmly answers "well no, I don't think we weren't allowed to talk to him, we just didn't did we?"

This was when my mind got blown! I could not believe her simple response to one of my strongest and most impressionable memories from my childhood from the Summer holidays spent in Ireland at grandma's house where the invisible man lived in the back room, and when he came out to use the bathroom or the kitchen we would all completely ignore him and pretend he wasn't there. How did she firstly, not even remember how totally fucked up that was? And secondly, how did she not know we weren't allowed to speak to him out of loyalty to grandma? And if this was the case, why had I been told, and she hadn't? Then that was when the penny finally dropped for me. My mother or grandma hadn't told me not to speak to him, they had 'shown' me not to speak to him. This gamechanger drove me to find out what that really meant. And what I found out changed everything.

I finally discovered I was 'highly sensitive' at the age of 37, and so I read everything I could find on highly sensitive people. Suddenly my whole life made sense! The intense feelings from a young age, the need to go deep and talk deep, why the horrible bits affected me so severely then and years later, why I felt 'everything' and why I was able to recall so many details and memories still to this day, the strong reaction to sudden loud noises or people creeping up on me or invading my space, preferring one on one company rather than groups of people, needing so much time and space on my own, especially after socials, the need to know the who, what, when and where of every situation so there were no surprises. It also explained why my brother and sister were not affected in the same way as me with our childhood, and why they couldn't really recall anything very well, because they were not highly sensitive. Which also explained why I was the only one throwing a tennis ball up against every wall whilst manically talking to myself!

I had to protect myself because I was under constant attack growing up because of my high sensitivity, and flippant comments from my mother such as "you were a mistake you know? we never really wanted you?" led me to feel a burden not just to my parents, but to every person in my life for the next 30 years. So, if you're highly sensitive too and you grew up in a house with all non-sensitive people, I feel your pain. That is a really tough gig. Because not only do you have to deal with all the emotions you have going on inside you, you have to deal with everyone else's too. Because if being highly sensitive wasn't enough, you are almost certainly an empath too. (Great eh?) Yep, you pick up on everybody else's feelings around you too. In fact you may as well have an antenna sticking out of your head the way other peoples' energy will flood you, and you won't have a clue as a kid that half the stuff you're feeling ain't even your own stuff. And that is how I knew I wasn't allowed to speak to my grandad out of loyalty to my grandma at the age of 4 years old and onwards, because I 'felt' from them that it was what they wanted me to do.

I believe that is why some people are able to fairly easily get over incredibly traumatic experiences in their life while others can't get past one nasty comment made in their childhood. Sometimes I wonder how differently my life would have turned out if I had had those colourfully wonderful parents I had read and written about in my very early childhood. What would I have turned out like if my highly sensitive side had been nurtured? But then I guess I wouldn't be writing this book now, would I?

After 'that conversation' I didn't say too much more to my sister, but the next time we met up, a few months later I said "hey, I hope I didn't upset you with what I said about our grandad?" and she said straight away, no hesitation "no no, I thought about it after you left actually, and yeah, I never really

thought about it before, but yes it was a bit like that wasn't it?''
I smiled gently, that meant a lot to me. She had given me
acknowledgement. I had always struggled to come to terms
with my relationship with my sister, it not being the way I
wanted it to be. I'd always wanted a tight strong bond with her,
but we just never had that. We were always distant strangers.
I'd hoped when we were older we could get it as I was sure she
must have felt the same way inside as I did, but just didn't want
to show that to me, but one day she would say "I feel the same
as you" and show me that side of her. But that never
happened. And now I get it, we are wired completely
differently. I was born highly sensitive and she wasn't, it's as
simple as that.

So, after I decided to switch my brain off as a child, I really don't
remember a lot about school, it's a bit of a blur and I really
don't think I learnt anything from there, nothing seemed to go
in. My mother began to lose control over me when I got to 13, I
was no longer fearful of her and I simply stopped caring what
she thought of me. I had got a good group of girl friends at
school, we called ourselves 'The A Team.' They had become my
peers and it was only their opinions that mattered to me. I went
a bit wild too, the usual stuff; smoking, drinking, drugs, boys. It
was scary looking back as because I had been so sheltered as a
child all I wanted to do was rebel, and rebel hard, and the
frightening thing was I had no boundaries. Home life became
utter hell, lots of arguing as my repressed anger started to roll
out to match my mother's repressed anger, saying hateful
things to one another. All I wanted was out of there. I ran away
from home when I was 14 with my best friend Sarah Taylor. We
had no real plan, we just packed a bag and headed off. We only
got 2 miles up the road and hung out in a playground for 5
hours. I can still remember the feeling I had when I threw my
bag on the ground and shouted internally 'I'm free' and the
pure elation of freedom rushing through my body. I really

wanted to keep going on the adventure, but Sarah got worried, then sad, then missed her mum, so we had to go back. I of course had the 'not so welcome home party' to deal with when I got home. After that day I knew I would have to wait until I was 16 to leave properly, when I couldn't be made to go back. And I did just that. I met a guy when I was 15 who was 26, and 3 months later when I turned 16, I left home and moved in with him. Now as you can probably guess he wasn't a good guy, and I began to realise why he couldn't get someone his own age. The abuse started early on, name calling, spitting on me, trying to suffocate me with a pillow. But because I had already experienced and endured a lot of abuse at home, which didn't actually feel much different from being spat on, I didn't let it bother me too much. I kind of thought that must have been what love was. After a while though it did become too much, and I no longer wanted to be there either, but even with all of the physical abuse I was suffering, it was still better than having to go home. I eventually got away from him properly when I was 20. I'd left a couple of times before and went and stayed with a friend, but he talked me into going back. But then one time I was taken to a women's refuge because my life was at risk from him, and when I got there it was packed out with a whole array of battered women. Young ones, old ones, ones with kids, ones without, and they all had a harrowing story to tell me. Because it was so busy there the woman on duty told me I would have to sleep on the sofa in the front room for the time being, but she reassured me that I didn't have to worry as the window was brick proof, so if anyone attempted to get in or make a point I'd be quite safe. Ok, so if I wasn't worried before this I was now, as I had only ever been worried about my crazy ex coming to attack me, but now I was worried about all the other women's crazy ex partners coming after them too and finding me first! I had also been led to believe the location of the refuge was a secret and everyone who stayed there had sworn an oath to not tell, I had even been driven there covertly. But the next morning a flower company turned up with a bunch of roses for one of the guests. So not so secret after all. As you will probably know being a highly sensitive empath, we seem to drink everybody in. I sat with the woman who had received the flowers and asked her what was going on, but I already knew before I even asked her, I could see the tiny smile on her face when she read the card and handled the bouquet that she would be back with him soon. It turned out it was her husband and she had been in this refuge 4 times before, and she'd been in hospital because of him a lot more than 4 times. What struck me the most was that she was in her 40's and seemed so self-assured by the way she carried herself. I couldn't understand why she would need to put herself through this same cycle of abuse over and over again, that was clearly never going to stop. Did she not know better? And it was meeting her that stopped my own cycle of abuse with my dangerous on and off boyfriend. I didn't want to end up like her, I wanted better for myself. So I left him for good and moved in with a friend. Because I never had any goals or dreams I just sort of fell into jobs. I blindly stumbled into a good job in recruitment when I was 23. I absolutely loved the people I worked with, and the feeling was mutual, it was the first time I felt like I was part of a family. They cared about me without wanting or expecting anything from me. I spent Christmases and birthdays at their houses with their families, they came with me to buy a new car and look at houses, we went out on day trips together and supported each other through relationship breakups, deaths and babies. I did really well at the job too for a couple of years and made good money, enough to buy a house. I was becoming a 'real person' I had a good job, I had money, I had good friends, I was happy. And because I was happy my creativity started to come back, I started reading and writing again. Life was great for a while. But the trouble was I still felt like that lost little girl inside, she hadn't gone away. I was just play acting at life, it wasn't really real, and I was hiding who I was from my new family. I didn't know how to handle being successful, it wasn't me, I didn't deserve it. I had just been lucky; it was a fluke and I would be called out as a fraud any day now and it would all be taken away from me. 'The Murrays have this sort of life, you don't.' My new family would then see I wasn't the special TJ that they all adored, they would see the ugly mess I really was. I had to stop reading and writing again. Alcohol was the only way I could deal with it, so I spent my 20s out most nights drunk, and I spent my 30s in most nights drunk. My social anxiety really started to wake up and kick in when I was around 25, so I left the job at 26 never keeping in contact with any of my new family.

I had to get a job working from home as I couldn't cope being around lots of people anymore. I was grateful to get something that kept me paying the bills just about, with the help of a lodger. The trouble was working from home was feeding my anxiety and allowing me to disappear from my life. I had years of dead-end relationships, a couple of long-term ones, but most never getting past 4 months. All adding to my opinion that I was unlovable and not able to fit in with someone. I spent years soul searching, trying to find the answers to help me. I tried everything; therapy, life coaching, CBT, NLP, tapping, self-help books, meditation, kinesiology, reiki, acupuncture, hypnotism. They gave me lots of answers but not the answer I was looking for.

Little did I know then how simple the answer actually was, and that once I found it, I would be happier than I could have ever imagined in my craziest wildest dreams. And that I would finally be able to stop running and hiding, and I would be free to be the real me. I only found it a couple of years ago.

So I guess I wanted to write this book to make your journey easier by giving you everything I have, and I have a lot, and if it helps just one other person who feels like I felt, then it will have been so worth it. I would love to hear from you to tell me what you do think, so feel free to email me at sparkstara@aol.com I love listening to other people's stories, and it would be lovely to hear from people who have similar feelings to me.

I hope it will be a help to whoever reads it, but I guess I especially wanted to reach out to the older people who may feel it's too late to change their life around. As I've read a lot of fantastic self-help books, but I've found in general the author will tend to say 'yeah I was depressed and at rock bottom for 3 whole years, then I finally sorted myself out at the grand old age of 27' which is great to hear, but for a lot of us we have lived a lifetime in depression, and I wanted to show you that I'm living proof that you can be depressed pretty much your whole existence and have your life on hold until you're nearly 40, and still manage to completely turn it around and become truly happy. I want that for you too, no matter how old you are I promise you can do it too, you can do it with me.

So, diving straight in! No time like the present eh?

Visualisation is one of the tools I want you to find, keep and use regularly. It's going to be instrumental in creating your new life, and if nothing else it is a great brain workout, and who doesn't need that?

Think back to what your childhood bedroom looked like. Picture it in your mind like you are there now. Go around the whole room in your mind, remembering what was there, beds, shelf units, what was on the shelf units? What posters did you have up on the wall? Try to recall some childhood memories. Did you have an imaginary friend? Did you like playing certain

games? Play around with it, just start to get an understanding of just how incredible your brain really is.

It's important for me to say not all of my childhood memories were bad. I had good ones too. I told you about how much I loved playing in the Wendy house at school. Well I have one really strong happy memory of me playing in that Wendy house on my own with the toy pots and pans on the plastic stove smiling away to myself. I often wonder what I was smiling about, was I thinking about something?

Kill Me Now

Ahhh the 'S' word. I hate it when people say 'they committed suicide' like it's a crime. Or should I say like it still is a crime. Because up until 1961 attempting suicide was a crime. So, if you survived your suicide attempt you would then be prosecuted and slung into prison! Now I am aware there are a few pity partiers out there who have no intention of taking their own life and just want a bit of attention from their loved ones, so they will glug a few pills down, not enough to do any real damage then call their rescuer for help. But I'm thinking the majority of suicidees *hey I made a new word* have probably been in a really crap place for a long time to want to do this. Then they decide to take the brave step (yes I said brave) to go through with it, and then to fail and have more misery, only then to be punished and shamed publicly, and used without consent as a deterrent for others contemplating the same action. It's just another example of control in our society. To keep us all in line and to keep us all singing from the same hymn sheet. *God, I hope they don't ever make us do that. Really not up for the hymns again.* Shame and guilt are the easiest and quickest ways to enforce that control, as shown with my parents and their parents. The biggest issue with suicide is that it has been made such a taboo subject. If you even mention the word the room goes quiet, and people stare with grave expressions on their faces, and usually change the subject at lightning speed to something far less serious. I remember many years ago a therapist asking me towards the end of our first session together if I had ever had suicidal thoughts? I glared utterly dumbfounded at her and thought to myself 'well bloody hell I've just sat here and told you all this messed up stuff that I have in my head, all the time going around and around, from the second I wake up until the second I manage to drop off at night and then find myself having nightmares about my life being even worse than it is now. How I am sick to death of hearing nasty comments about me in my head constantly. How I am filled to the brim with emotions I can't deal with, how tears start rolling down my face every time I go out driving. How I feel worthless, and on edge permanently, and have to drink alcohol everyday as soon as I finish work. How lonely I feel because I can never be truly with someone, and how I'll never have a child of my own because I don't want to risk passing the burden batten on to them, and I wouldn't be able to cope with them anyway. How I feel uncomfortable in my own skin all of the time, and know that I'm not a 'real person' and how gut wrenching shit it is to be around normal happy people who are constantly making plans and moving forwards in their lives and telling me all about it, and I just have to stand there and say wow that's great, and when they start asking about my plans I have to lie and divert the conversation back to them because I haven't got any plans or goals, as there doesn't seem any point. How I have to hide the fact that I'm just made up and held together by very loose sticky tape that I know is going to fall apart any minute, and everyone will gasp in horror at the liquified incoherent mess before them, and they will wonder how on earth did I let myself get into this state. How I hate the fact that I have to wear black all the time because of the sweating. How tiring it is to have to drag my body around with me all day long because it has zero motivation all of the time, and I'm permanently drained and exhausted, and I haven't showered for the last 3 days because it's too much effort. And how I have been stuck down the bottom of a black hole for so long I can't even remember what the light looks like, I'm not even sure I have ever seen it.

So yes! Of course I've fucking thought about topping myself, you mentalist!' She carries on before I am able to answer her inane question and says, 'because I need to inform your doctor if this is the case'. In case you're wondering, I told her no, I never had any suicidal thoughts, I left and never went back. She may well have had my best interests at heart and was genuinely worried for me, but once you get the feeling your therapist is more interested in covering their own arse than letting you speak your truth there's little point in going back as trust is paramount with a therapist. And I knew from that moment I couldn't be honest with her, because the real honest truth was I'd not only thought about suicide, I'd started to plan it, and not just once, but several times.

I never 'wanted' to kill myself. I think that's what bugs me the most when people who have no idea about being in this situation try to vilify you by calling you selfish. The thought of killing myself made me feel physically sick. If I could have just been able to press a button and disappear forever, even better still just have had my whole existence wiped out from that press of a button, so nobody would miss me or be affected by my death, I would have done it in a heartbeat. But it's not that simple is it? You have to come up with a plan, and on your own too because you can't get advice from your mates on which way is the best. And the options available aren't great. You've either got to down loads of pills and probably get your stomach viciously pumped later, and then feel guilty about wasting the nurses, doctors and paramedics time and energy. Jump in front of a train? Which I think would be the quickest way, but I've been on 4 or 5 trains where it has been delayed for several hours because of a jumper, usually on a Friday because they've had a bad week and don't want to spend another weekend completely alone with only their wretched thoughts for company. But the commuters never get that. All they see is the inconvenience of it; missed job interviews, missed train connections, holiday delays, arguments with loved ones because they're in such a shitty mood by the time they get off the train. I would hate to cause that knock-on effect to so many people, now that would be pretty selfish. Slit the wrists? This one makes me too squeamish, I really don't like the sight of blood, especially my own. Hang yourself? I can't even begin to think about that one. For me I'd have to somehow make it look like an accident, mainly so my mother wouldn't suffer unbearable pain. Not unbearable pain from losing her daughter of course, but unbearable pain from the shame she would have to endure because of it. Which I know would be far greater than any grief she would experience. I think my father would be ok about it. I have my suspicions he may have contemplated it himself a few times by playing the absent a.k.a. busy father routine. And what if those attempts didn't work? Are you going to be even worse afterwards, like paralysed, not able to speak or do anything to escape it, and knowing you'll never have the chance to try it again? Surely the worst part of that would be having the people around you knowing what you'd tried to do. Shit, the shame. How do you explain that? When the whole world just sees you as the 'warm and cheerful' one? Christ how can that even be possible? Are people that blind, or am I just that good at hiding who I really am? It's a total and utter headfuck. It's like playing a long running tv soap character who everyone loves but they don't want to know the actual person playing the role. I feel like roadkill, yet here I am making other people crack up with laughter from my jokes. And what happens if you are successful with your attempt, and you do end up on the other side? Well what if the other side is even worse? And by opting out of this life means you failed 'the test' and you just get frozen in time feeling exactly how you do now for eternity. Or you might get sent straight back to earth as a newborn baby with an even shittier life in store for you. So, for all these reasons this is how I know the people that do go through with suicide are incredibly brave, as they will have experienced all of these thoughts and feelings for an exceptionally long time. How dare these misinformed 'know it all' fuckwits dare to say 'it's a coward's way out' WTH? I'd like to see them cope with all that head noise whilst trying to plan a get out strategy all on their own! Or another good one is the 'guilt trip.' 'There's all these people suffering in the world who would kill to swap places with you, so you should realise how lucky you are!' Yeah again, really lucky to feel like roadkill 247! And the biggest rock thrown in the continuing mental stoning 'how could they do it to the people they love?' Wow! It's a huge misconception that suicidees are too far gone at that moment to think about their loved ones when they go through the exit. In fact that's one of the main reasons they go through, because they don't want to be a burden on the people they love. They want them to be free from their all-consuming negative dark cloud presence, and to go on and have a much happier life released from them. I remember there was a program on television a few years ago about a woman who died at the age of 38 in her North London flat but wasn't discovered until 2 years later. People were stunned when they watched it, as they could not believe something like that could happen in modern society. The people who had known the woman when she was in her 20s spoke on the show about her, how she was beautiful inside and out, and the life and soul of the party, and was a joy to be around, and lit up every room she walked into. Which made it even more confusing for the audience to grasp her unnoticeable death. How can a 38-year-old popular woman just die and have no family or friends to know she was gone for 2 whole years? But I totally got it. She basically committed the next best thing to physical suicide, 'emotional suicide' she cut everyone off. The people on the show hadn't seen her for about 10 years before her death. She appeared to have just slowly drifted away from everyone, and they presumed she was busy living a fabulous life somewhere. But she wasn't. She had cut them off and disappeared from her own life. You see it's seen as acceptable in your 20's to flaunt around aimlessly and party all the time like the eternal child with no proper life plan. People will actually admire you for being so carefree and fun, and will want to be around you, partying with you. But then these same people expect you to see that the party has ended and calm down by 30 and become a 'proper person' with a partner and a serious career, with goals and plans, and live in a nice house with lots of nice stuff in it to show you know what grown-ups spend their money on. This is the program that everyone is supposed to follow and follow it you must. So, if you ignore the program and you never really grow up and haven't achieved anything solid that people can witness, or have zero plans to do so, you will feel a complete failure and want to hide away so nobody can see that you fucked up. You can even have all the fine trimmings in life; big house, fancy cars, champagne bar in your basement, and still feel a failure if you're not emotionally following the program. So I totally get why you would slowly start cutting people off, and if you persevere enough, after a while even people who care very much about you will eventually give up trying if you push them away enough. In my mind she had been seen as such a charismatic soul who lit up the world and rocked every room she entered when she was showing herself that she didn't want to 'not be seen as that' anymore. She didn't want to deal with the endless questioning on what she was doing now and how had she become even more remarkable. It's like Marilyn Monroe, she overdosed at age 36, so she died as a huge culture icon, beautiful and breathtakingly fabulous. You'll never be able to think of her in any other way. This is the same for regular people who decide to take their own life. They want to leave while they still have some fucking dignity left, because it's disappearing fast. I've felt this pressure myself. I've found nearly everyone I meet is instantly drawn to my highly sensitive nature when I have it out on show. It's like a beacon that is calling them to talk to me, because they instinctively know I will really hear and feel what they are telling me. They say to me things like 'You're really interesting to talk to, I feel so much better having talked to you, you should become a therapist.' It used to be a massive part of my anxiety throughout my life, as I felt pressure to keep this performance up and to become the person they had such strong admiration for.

I think a lot of people suffering with suicidal thoughts are freaked out by the apparent sudden downslope of depression and anxiety they experience. Which can make us believe we were living the good life beforehand, with strong healthy feelings and good self-esteem, and that out of nowhere this asteroid of misery came hurtling towards us and hit us right on the head and quickly started destroying our lives and tearing apart everything we had built up. The reality in most cases is that our lives weren't that great to begin with. And we had probably started feeling like this since early childhood, but we learned to block the feelings out with coping mechanisms, and as we got older, we found ways to distract ourselves with addictions, work and relationships. Then one day our minds and bodies simply had enough of feeling so rubbish and pretending everything was alright all of the time when it was far from alright. And they started acting out and playing up to get your attention to say 'hey, you, we're not happy and we ain't putting up with this bullshit any longer so sort it out.' When we realise that this is the real story, we can start to see it as an opportunity to be really honest with ourselves about why we are feeling so low and anxious. We can delve into our past that we have covered up for so long and start to see the destructive patterns we are living out time and time again. The learnt harmful behaviour from our parents we are carrying out subconsciously in our everyday life. We need to realise that most of us only operate on about 10% of our brains every day (the conscious) the other 90% (the subconscious) is doing its own thing all of the time. Which if you've had unresolved trauma in your past you can be sure it's going to be playing the 'worsted hits of your childhood' over and over in the background. It was very liberating for me to realise that my anxiety and depression didn't actually start at 25 like I first thought, it had been there for all my life. That was why I never had a purpose in life, why all my relationships with men left me feeling either rejected (mother) or abandoned. (father) I had gone through a never ending cycle of being miserable and wanting to end it all, to meeting someone shiny and new who in the beginning would give me what I so desperately craved in my life, so I would feel life was worth living again, to it ending badly because I was so out of touch with my feelings that I couldn't give it back to them, to feeling miserable, once again.

You will probably feel incredibly sad when you realise you first started feeling this way not as an adult but as a child, so take some time to acknowledge and cry for that little version of you, they went through an awful lot to get you to here, today. But then when you feel ready, move your focus away from them and onto the amazing opportunity you now have to really start living to your full potential. You now know what you're really dealing with here, so you can start to change it. We were never given the tools to deal with it in our childhood, but it doesn't matter, because we're going to get those tools ourselves, now.

We live in a time where it is all about 'individualism.' Gone is the community spirit and working as a collective. Everyone wants to be relevant, unique and extraordinary. It is not enough anymore to be just a regular person with a regular job. You either have to look like a supermodel and have a super jet set lifestyle to match, or be a philanthropist, humanitarian, motivational speaker who runs 5 charities and saves the world on a daily basis. People invest so much time and energy into their own marketing on social media. Even ordinary people have to spend a large amount of their free time on their social media accounts, adding photos of their awesome experiences to prove that their avatar is having a good time. 'Reserved' and 'mild' are considered nauseating negative traits. You need to have a larger than life 'look at me, look at me again' personality to be popular. Did you know the word personality didn't even exist until the 18th century? And having a good personality didn't come about until the 1900's. Before the rise of 'good personalities' people were admired for being serious and practical. It was only when people began working on their personalities that the extrovert appeared, and quickly took centre stage with their loud 'I say it like it is' style. Nowadays it is all about how many countries you've travelled to, how great your career is, and how amazing your body looks from all the gym sessions you are managing to squeeze in. Our egos are completely running the show. Which is why social media creates so much bloody misery, as it's not based on anything real, just ego. There is a real crisis on our hands today with people suffering from serious FOMO and feeling inadequate from spending too much time on social media. The real truth is NONE OF IT IS REAL. They only show you the good parts and hide the bad. A good friend of mine who had a very successful high flying career once told me she was incredibly mentally unwell when she was going through the menopause for a couple of years and really wanted to end her life by ramming her car into a brick wall, *ouch!* and spent most of her time crying in bed but all the while posting on social media about how spectacular her life was and how happy it made her. That's the thing, it isn't actually you they want to convince they are having a great time, it's themselves. Think about it, if you were having such an amazing time on holiday in the Caribbean you wouldn't even think about stopping to post about it, you would be too absorbed in the immensely satisfying adventure you were physically experiencing, totally detached from technology. The same goes for social influencers, they can only exist with your attention, they need you more than you need them. So never take too much notice of social media posts, take what you see and read with a pinch of salt. *Pinch of salt? I am going to take a break and look up where that saying comes from.*

The other giant problem is that we are never allowed to be our authentic selves, which is hard if you are highly sensitive. It's like when people in the UK ask us how we are we, and we say, 'Oh I'm fine thank you, how are you?' Well according to Aerosmith FINE stands for fucked up, insecure, neurotic, emotionally unstable. Which pretty much answers the how are you question for most people today. Nearly everyone I know is on anti-depressants. What sort of world do we live in where most of us are taking happy pills? The doctors literally dish them out like sweeties. And I wouldn't mind if they did actually work, but they don't. They usually end up blocking all of a person's feelings, so they end up feeling like they are living their life as a zombie stuck behind a Perspex screen where nothing seems real anymore. Anxiety and depression have become an epidemic. And we can no longer ignore it.

That's why suicide always seemed the obvious choice to me, to escape this 'one size fits all' horseshit. I actually think it's really weird that other people don't contemplate suicide. I mean life can be pretty mundane and crappy, even for the ones following the life program. Doing the same tedious job day in day out that you absolutely hate, staying in a relationship with someone you don't even like that much anymore because you don't want to be alone and you need them to help pay that silly big mortgage you took out. I see them in restaurants all the time, these so called happily committed couples, who manage to go through the entire meal without uttering a single word to one another. How can they never question it? I don't get it. It's odd, really fucking odd to just go along with it because everyone else does. There are people out there who don't even know what a self-help book is let alone ever picked one up. Mindlessly having loads of children because it's 'what you do' never-mind the state of the planet already due to overpopulation. They choose to ignore the elephant in the room. But it's too much for us isn't it, as highly sensitive people? We cannot ignore the feelings of dissatisfaction from the program.

A lot of people will also say 'well they were ill, that's why they did it' because they want a solid sound explanation for suicide. Something that they can understand without having to really understand, and they can give it a label so it can then be filed away under 'mental health issue.' Now that is true in some part that yes obviously their mental health wasn't working as well as it should be, but the person wasn't just happily going along in life then suddenly caught 'mental illness' so topped themselves. It's so much deeper than that, and it's only when you've been to the bottom of that black hole yourself that you'll ever understand that.

So, if we were allowed to talk openly about suicide, I believe we could really start making a difference for everyone, not just the ones who want to do it.

Trust me I NEVER thought I'd turn things around. It took me a painful breakup from 'The One' about 3 years ago which left me homeless with nothing to show for myself to get my arse in gear. I finally understood that trying to live a life as somebody else was never going to work. I had to start living 'my way'. So, I started simply. I stopped listening to my head and started listening to what my gut was telling me, and I took those steps. I then discovered an incredible process I call 'following the flow' (so incredible I have written a chapter on it later) which led me to find the thing I was looking for, the holy grail, the answer.

Concentrate for a moment and start thinking back. Delve into your past. How is your past affecting your actions now? What learned behaviour from your parents have you been using up

until now? What harmful programs are you running in your everyday life? Where do they come from?

So well done for making it this far, not just with the book but with your life, because if you have been feeling like I felt then you have endured far more than you should ever have to. And none of it has been your fault, it's just a by-product of the program. Life isn't meant to be that hard, it's meant to be glorious. So let me throw a rope down to you in that black hole and pull you out of there by sharing with you the answer.

The L Word

Ahhh the L word. It's a word that's sloshed about and around all over the place these days. We say it to our families, *well not my family* we say it to our friends and our partners. It's the inspiration for most songs we hear. We see it played out in nearly every film we watch. People kill and die for it. It's the thing we desire the most in life, and if you don't have it in your life, then you're not alive. Pretty damn essential to our human living experience then? But do you know what it is? Yes, it's 'LOVE' of course, but I mean do you know what 'love' actually is? You can't see it, so how do you know if you're loved by someone? It's a feeling, right? So, the big question is 'do you love yourself?' If we can only tell love is there by feeling it, do you have that feeling of love from yourself? I'm going to take a stab in the dark here and say that the answer to that question is no. You are probably so out of touch with your feelings that I'm thinking you probably aren't even aware that you don't love yourself. I think as humans we tend to naturally assume that 'loving yourself' is already stored in our factory settings. That it was put in there before we were born, along with all our other cognitive functions such as breathing and blinking. *Damn it, now I am aware of my blinking.* But sadly, this is simply incorrect. Loving ourselves is something we need to be taught, and learn, and us ourselves need to put it into our systems. And if you came from a dysfunctional family who didn't love themselves, well they couldn't possibly teach you to do it and pass on to you how vitally important it is for your wellbeing. And the saying goes 'if you don't love yourself how can you possibly love someone else?' I can tell you now that no relationship you will have in your life will ever be more important than the one you have with yourself. Romantic love is not guaranteed and can stop existing at any given moment, it is conditioned; I will keep loving you if you only ever have eyes for me, if you are there for me when I need you, and if you put the bins out every week.

However, the love that you give to yourself is completely unconditional and totally limitless. You can love yourself forever, NO MATTER what you do or don't do. You can have the ultimate love affair, with yourself. You can be your one true love, never giving up on yourself, being there all the time for yourself through thick and thin, forgiving yourself when you've done something wrong, picking yourself up when you've failed, supporting your dreams and goals, being your own rock. I understand now why none of my previous relationships ever worked out, because I never loved them, nor could I love them, because I didn't even know what love was. All the time and money I had spent on different types of therapy when the one thing that would actually work was completely free, and I didn't even have to leave my house or turn my computer on to obtain it. Now you may be thinking 'yeah yeah, heard that hippy crap before, no way is it as easy as that, just give me a magic pill instead.' Well I'm not saying it's easy, far from it actually. Loving yourself takes hard work and full commitment. And like all relationships it will be extremely uncomfortable at times for you. You will lose friends because your priorities will change, so then in turn the dynamics of those relationships will change. You may have to change your job or where you live because everything in your life will come into question. You will completely change as a person. And that is a bit distressing isn't it, living a life of the unknown? Yeah, you're unhappy now in your life, but you know it well and you know what to expect living this way don't you? As I touched on earlier, it's not failure that scares us the most, it's success, because we don't know how to handle it and live up to it.

It's why so many people that have a lot of money and fame can easily become depressed, and abuse themselves with drugs and alcohol, because the money and fame isn't capable of making them happy. Happiness is a feeling inside. Money is an external substance we use to obtain stuff with. But buying physical items doesn't make us happy, we might be fooled into thinking it does for a while, but happiness is a state of mind, and you don't need to be rich or famous or have 500 thousand followers online to get into that state. Anyone can move into that state, but it takes understanding and dedication. I've seen it time and time again with rich people I've known who have all the 'stuff' but are either bored and depressed, or angry and resentful, compared to low earners I've known who are extremely positive, fulfilled and content. If a person feels they have a true purpose in life even if they are not paid very well, they will always be much more fulfilled in their life. It's why a lot of lottery winners still turn up to their 9-5 minimum wage job and why billionaires still work 50 hours a week, because they still need a purpose to get up in the morning. Other people scoff at them and say 'well if I had all that money I can tell you now I wouldn't work another day in my life,' but in reality they would become empty real quick, you need to see that. It's awesome attracting money in a healthy way by doing things that will make you feel good inside, but as the money pot grows don't forget who you are and what your purpose is. And that you need to keep growing as a person to keep that magic going, because it's the magic that gives you the good feelings, not the money itself.

Not loving myself held me back in my life in so many ways, mainly because I didn't believe in myself. I never believed I was capable of anything. Anything I did achieve I put down to luck or fluke. I never claimed these wins as my own, so I was never fulfilled. I always wanted to write and loved doing so, but I could never bring myself to try to get my work published as I never believed it would be good enough for that. I never even tried because I had convinced myself with a belief. I let myself believe the cruel lie that The Murrays were more deserving than me, and somehow naturally better and more equipped at living life than me. Not loving yourself will leave you incapable of doing **anything** with your life. You will never realise what you are good at. You will never realise what your dreams are. You will never set goals to achieve those dreams. You will never feel satisfaction or fulfilment with anything that you do accomplish, and you will never have wholesome relationships with other people; romantically or platonically. It's hard to hear all of that I Know, but the good news is that when you do start loving yourself, right now, just as you are now, you do start believing in yourself. And you will find out what you are good at, and what your passions are, and that you are without any doubt capable and deserving of achieving whatever you want in your life. And suddenly one day soon you start going after those dreams like a huge unstoppable freight train, and you start making your dreams reality.

The first thing you need to understand about the human mind is that there are 2 parts to it: the conscious and the sub conscious. Your conscious is the surface side of your mind where you have all the daily thinking and decision making. And where 'Neggy Nagbag' lives, which is my nickname for the annoying negative nagging voice in my head. The subconscious is the deep side of your mind where everything you think consciously throughout the day gets churned around and usually gives you some pretty freaky dreams that night. You are never really aware of the subconscious as when we are awake, we are conscious. You only become aware of the subconscious when you are going into sleep state like daydreaming or just before you drop off at night. If you have ever been hypnotised or have ever seen someone else be hypnotised, you will get an idea of just how susceptive the brain is to hypnotic commands. The brain has been put into that pre sleep state when they are hypnotised, so the hypnotist is talking directly to the sub conscious from then on. The conscious mind is temporarily dormant so it cannot halt the hypnotist's outrageous suggestions such as 'you are now a chicken' or 'you have lost your car keys.' The audience then get a thrill out of seeing the hypnotised person act out the role of being a human flapping chicken or scrambling around the stage frantically looking for their car keys. The subconscious mind simply acts out what it is being told, it doesn't question if it is real or not, the sub conscious is not rational. So, with this in mind start realising the vast potential you have in that subconscious mind of yours, and that what you tell it with your conscious mind the subconscious will start to act out for you. As I mentioned before the sub conscious is 90% of our minds. So that's a hell of a lot of untapped power within ourselves that we are ignoring. The easiest way to understand and tap into it is to think of the subconscious as a big green lawned garden, and your conscious mind as the gardener of that green lawned garden, who starts to plant stuff on the lawn throughout the day. The plants are your thoughts. If you have bad negative thoughts about yourself throughout the day then you will be planting weeds all day long on the lovely green lawn, and those weeds will spread until eventually you can no longer see the green lawn, only huge ugly weeds, and it will be a total mess and too much for you to sort out. However if you have good positive thoughts throughout the day, you will be planting beautiful flowers on that lovely green lawn, and the flowers will flourish and spread, and there will be vibrant colours and aromas in your garden galore, and it will be a joy to spend time there. I didn't realise I had been planting weeds in my garden my whole life starting from when I was a child. Telling myself at age 4 to stop learning as it was bad for me. Telling myself I wasn't good enough, that everyone else was better than me, that I was useless, worthless and pointless. All these poisonous negative thoughts and beliefs about myself were weeds going into my garden. It took me until my late 30's to start planting flowers, but because my garden was so overgrown, I had to do some serious de-weeding. We have to kill off those weeds; the old negative false beliefs we have in our heads, by pushing them out with so many flowers; new positive helpful beliefs, that there simply isn't any room for weeds to grow. You have to understand though it takes hard work and full commitment to get your mind into shape before you can start using it beneficially. When people suddenly decide out of the blue they are going to give up smoking or take up running, they will convince themselves they can do it because the thought of accomplishing it makes them feel really good, unfortunately they don't go the right way about it. They will just start telling themselves 'I'm going to quit smoking' or 'I'm going to run every day starting tomorrow.' They believe it's all down to willpower. But they don't grasp that willpower comes from the conscious part of your mind, so you are only working with 10% straightaway. So, no wonder they fail so easily and never even get past the first day of their challenge, and they end up getting disheartened that 'being positive' doesn't work. It's why New Year's resolutions never really work because you are just telling your subconscious a command a few times during the day, and though you are really strong and determined when you say it, your subconscious mind isn't paying much attention, and is just filtering it out with all the other rubbish because it doesn't recognise it as being important to you. You need to speak directly to your subconscious, and not just in thoughts or words, you need to visualise what it is you want too, and you need to embrace the 'feeling' you get from that visualisation technique and stay in that feeling so that you feel you have already accomplished your new goal. This will really get your subconscious mind's attention and get it actively involved, but you will be in charge of it, not the other way around. The best time to do it is when you are drowsy just before you drop off at night and first thing in the morning before you are properly awake. When you fool your subconscious mind into believing you have already achieved something and are feeling good about it, it will inevitably make it happen for you as it believes it already has done so.

We also need to take back control of our conscious brain that has been hijacked long ago from external sources such as tv, radio and advertisement companies. Our brains are constantly downloading every single thing we hear and see, it is ALL going into our subconscious. My partner has a habit of singing or humming a couple of lines from a song throughout the day and sometimes I won't be consciously listening, as I'll be zoned out cooking or something, but then the next minute I am singing that song out loud and then I suddenly stop and think why am I singing that? We need to start being mindful of what we are seeing and hearing, and not just let ourselves zone out and take in harmful data that our subconscious mind doesn't know what to do with. We take back control in stages, where we become more and more mindful everyday of what we are truly seeing and hearing, until we eventually become the master of our own minds. We need to start to do it in the physical world too so that our bodies match our minds. This means making decisions 'ourselves' in our lives and no longer being a passenger in someone else's car being driven wherever they want to go. The driver of that car could be your partner, friends, acquaintances, boss, parent, television, social media. There are huge corporations out there that make a lot of money having you interested in their products, so they usually use some pretty unscrupulous methods to get you hooked on them. They are not interested in your wellbeing, they just want to generate money from you, that is all. Television studios and film companies are no different. They want you watching their creations, their babies, by showing you people leading exciting and unpredictable lives to convince you that it's more interesting for you to watch their lives play out on screen than to turn the tv off and put that interest into your own potentially exciting life. This is another danger of not loving ourselves, we tend not to have any real direction in life, so we can look to others to give us the answers and let them lead us. Whilst it is great to gain knowledge and experience from people we admire, we must make sure we are the ones driving the car. Remember you are the gardener of that green lawn. Nobody else can be your gardener. Therapists, life coaches and even doctors will not invest in you as much as you are able to. I'm sure a lot of them really do care about their work, but they have many many clients/patients to give their time and energy to, which is why they have to keep notes on you. And also, it's their job that they are getting paid for. So, while getting a bit of help from these experienced people can be extremely beneficial and supportive, never give them sole responsibility of sorting your problems and your life out for you, as they will inevitably come up short. **You** however can invest absolutely everything into your wellbeing, it can be your life's work if you let it. Be your own best friend. If you are highly sensitive then you are already immensely caring and supportive of others, and it's a sad fact that the only person who isn't benefiting from your caring nature at the moment is 'you.' So, start getting selfish and putting yourself first in that queue, and start pouring that immense care and support into yourself. Start telling yourself good things about yourself all day long and congratulate yourself for at least 3 things a day that you have achieved. It doesn't matter how small or how silly they seem, just do it. And don't let others neg you out or talk down to you.

When I became mindful, I started to become aware that when I was out and about with someone else, I would automatically let them go first when we were walking anywhere. This was obviously harmful to my subconscious as my physical actions were telling it I wasn't a leader, and that I always needed to be shown the way by someone else. So from that moment onwards I made a point of making my body move in front of them. At first it felt awkward and uncomfortable, but I soon got used to it as we do with most repetitive habits. I stopped letting other people make decisions for me too, I started to trust my own judgements and stand by them. The more control you take of your daily life the more in control you will feel in general. Choose now to love yourself and start spending quality time with yourself, not sat on your phone texting or zoning out to mindless television. Meditate, watch motivational and inspirational feel good videos, get to know who you are and what you really want out of life. (winning the lottery is not an option btw) Do yoga, make plans to start some hobbies, read books, listen to audiobooks, enrol in some further education classes; there are plenty of very affordable and short (5 hours) online courses to get you started. Just start putting the time in and connect with yourself. It won't be long until you start getting the rewards from loving yourself. One sure sign that you are starting to love yourself is when you start challenging yourself. As then you are no longer looking outward for attention and admiration because that just doesn't cut it for you anymore, you want it from yourself. As you know that is going to get you the magic feeling you've been craving and missing out on your whole life, and give you that sense of pride you've been seeking for a very long time.

Now start feeding that subconscious mind of yours and start the love process in the most incredibly simple way. Tell yourself you love yourself, daily. Do it first thing in the morning. Do it while you are in the shower. Do it while you are on the bus or driving. Do it whenever wherever, as much as you can. Let those words absorb into you; 'I love myself.' A really powerful way to do this is to combine the affirmation with music, as music speaks to us on a different frequency and we are more open to our feelings when we listen to music. So, pick a song or piece of music that affects you deeply, you can probably think of a couple straightaway? Then listen to the song and let yourself feel it and then start saying the affirmation 'I love myself' over and over and let the feeling of pure undiluted love flow through every part of you. Although this is a very simple technique requiring very little action from you, **do not** underestimate the powerful effects it will make in your world. And those effects will happen instantly. The world around you will start to shift to fit your new frequency of love, radiating from your core. People will smile at you more, people will take more notice of you, people will be drawn to you, random good things will start happening for you. Then when you start feeling these effects try other sentences; 'My body feels really calm' is a good one for anxiety. Just repeat it over and over. I used to do this one quite a lot when I was out and about, as sometimes just a simple pleasant walk can turn ugly if you have negativity running through your mind. Anxiety sufferers tend to have stiff bodies and hold their shoulders up and feel awkward so are not sure what to do with their arms or hands, so just by telling yourself you are calm changes the way you hold your body and you will relax, and 10 minutes into it your arms will be swinging freely by your sides. Yes, it will feel bizarre at first, babbling random announcements in your head to your body and mind, but hey it's better than the usual nonsense swirling around in there isn't it? Plus talking to yourself will eventually get you to become more aware of those negative comments you have going on in your mind throughout the day and repetitive thoughts that hound you and ruin your day. Have you ever stopped and listened to what's going around in your head? Try it, don't intervene on or judge the thoughts, just let them come and go freely, and just watch them as a spectator, it's unbelievable guff. So, with your new useful healthy thoughts you can start to drown the neggy ones out until they finally get the hint and leave. Let your thoughts shrink for a while so the world gets bigger for you. Once you have a good hold on drowning out the negative thoughts then you can start using your mind for what it was really meant to do... **Create.** This is when you let your mind start expanding again, but this time it's in a cool way. This is when you will start seeing miracles and synchronicities in your life that you cannot explain with logic, and you will then realise you are way more powerful than you ever imagined. You will realise you are making stuff come true. You will realise you are a 'creator'. You've probably heard about the law of attraction? Well basically your mind needs to be in the right vibration to 'create' and the right vibration is the receiving mode of 'gratitude.' When you are in the receiving mode everything becomes easy there, as there is no resistance, or fear or worry, because you are already grateful for whatever you have right then and there, and your soul is open and receptive, asking for more of this please. So, in a nutshell; you think positive, you get positive. You think negative, you get negative.

Just watch how many doors suddenly open for you when you're practising gratitude. As you already expect the good things you want to happen, so inevitably they will manifest for you. You just have to sit back and trust they will happen and carry on being happy and grateful in your life exactly as it is. The key thing here is 'trust' which comes down to belief in the process. And you can only have belief in the process if you have belief in yourself, as if you don't believe in yourself as previously mentioned you won't feel deserving of everything the universe has waiting for you. And how do you truly believe in yourself? Yep, you learn to love yourself. Can you see how vital the L word is to everything now? Practising gratitude is so effortless too. You can be grateful for the tiniest incident that happens; someone letting you out of a busy junction in your car, someone giving you their carpark ticket because they've put way more time on there than they actually need, someone letting you go first in the queue at the supermarket cos you've only got a couple of items in your basket. This makes you realise just how many things there are to be grateful for every day. Like

I love when I get money off something I really want. I don't know why but I feel really good if I get a bargain, so I always say a little thank you for that. Or when I drive into a very busy carpark and there is just one space left, when you are grateful it really feels like that space was left especially for you. Or when a synchronicity happens, like I have my eye on a newly released expensive book in the store and I think I might treat myself and get that soon, then that same day I go for a massage treatment with the same lovely lady I have been going to for a few years so we have become quite friendly, and she just says out of the blue to me "oh I bought this new book, it's a really good read and I was thinking you would like it too. Would you like to borrow it?" Yep, it's the book I had my eye on in the store. I always chuckle and say thank you very much for these little divine moments. You cannot buy these moments with money. They are created by you and the universe working together.

Surrounding yourself with positive happy people who love themselves will aid you in loving yourself too, and you will feel happy and positive when you are around them. Unfortunately when we don't love ourselves we tend to attract the wrong people into our lives, as the law of attraction works both ways, if you are not in a good place you will attract other people who are not in a good place either. And you may not even recognise they are like this, as they can come across healthy at first. But you start to notice little things that they do; the nasty little comments they make about other people including their friends, (and trust me if they are bitching about all their other friends to you then you can be damn sure they are bitching about you to them also) the snidey passive aggressive behaviour directed at you if you're not behaving as they want you to. If you're also highly sensitive as well as not practising self-love, then I'll be very surprised if you haven't already got several emotional vampires as friends. They are attracted to you instantly once they pick up on your high sensitivity, because they know you will listen and empathize far more than the average person does. And boy have they got a lot of problems and dramas to tell you about! And once they realise you also have low self- esteem and that you are a people pleaser, well it's like their Christmases and birthdays have all come at once! You'll listen intently to all their problems and take them on as your own, and you'll keep coming back for more if they ask you to! They will suck the life out of you if you let them and they will walk away feeling lighter and energised for getting everything off their chest and stealing your lovely energy, and you'll be left emotionally battered and bruised wondering what the fuck just happened?!

Don't worry if you don't have any of the happy positive people in your life at the moment, just use your visualisation tool to imagine yourself surrounded by new friends and do this every night. Use your sessions in your subconscious to attract these glorious new friends. Imagine in your visualisation how it would be with these new friends. What you would be doing together. How would you be acting around them. How would you be feeling with them. And again, really feel that feeling while you are lying there visualising, let your subconscious know that this is the right feeling for you and that this is what you expect to happen.

I said earlier about being selfish and putting yourself first, which if you are highly sensitive and a people pleaser this takes a while to get your head around, as we are almost programmed to put others first and sort all their shit out. I literally could not cope with someone not liking me before I loved myself, even if I was never going to see that person again. The irony is you need to be selfish with your mental well-being to be able to properly help people, as you can't do it if you are a wreck yourself from over giving and drained from emotional vamps. From analysing people, I have come into contact with over the years I came to see so many people do love themselves and therefore put themselves first and feel absolutely no shame in it. And a lot of them weren't particularly nice people, but they didn't really care an awful lot what other people thought, it only seemed to matter what they thought about themselves. My ex partner's stepfather was one of these not particularly nice people, *just tell them what you really call him, they won't be offended. Tell them he was a complete 'c u next Tuesday'* and I honestly couldn't stand him, and unluckily for me he really liked me, so he would take me off for chats when we visited. Although I dreaded these amazingly draining dull one sided conversations, I cannot deny the value they taught me, that you can be a truly dreadful person but still love yourself and manage to find someone who's crazy enough to marry you. He absolutely thrived on confrontation because he saw it as an opportunity to win at something. He would boast to me about how much money he had made from his most recent con, and how many people he had crushed to get it. I'm pretty sure that saying 'how do you sleep at night?' started from one of his victims. People would literally cross the street to avoid him when we were out, he had no friends. None of that mattered to him though because he believed in himself and he was happy and wealthy. I remember I asked him once what he thought happiness was, and he told me happiness was a state of mind and that he would be happy even if he was in prison because he had the right mindset, and he felt he would probably find a way of making some money while he was in there. It showed me people that are successful, wealthy and happy aren't necessarily nice kind humans who deserve it all. So just remember that when you are hero worshipping, that these people are not super model humans who are better than you. You can have success and wealth too if you really want that, if you choose to believe in yourself as much as they believe in themselves. I understand now that it's ok if people don't like you, and that it's such a huge waste of time and energy trying to make people like you. It's ok to have faults, as long as you recognise them and work on them and still be kind to yourself. Nobody can make you feel bad or ridicule you if you already know your own faults and issues and you are working on them. And when you love yourself you will naturally start standing up for yourself more, and care less about impressing people. You also don't need to tell people everything about you or tell them everything you think, you say what you are comfortable with and that's all. Other people in your life will not always have your best interests at heart, and that can be for lots of reasons, but not always intentionally. There's a lot of very unhappy people out there and a lot are disguised as happy functioning folk. But because they are unhappy underneath they will not be happy if you start to do well in your life, because your success highlights their failures, and they won't like the feeling they get from that, and will probably do some underhand shit to try and mess you up. Just be aware of that, it doesn't make them evil masterminds. It's because they are unhappy, but don't let them drag you down there with them. It's understanding that negative comments say more about the person making them than the comment itself. People who are truly happy in themselves don't need to constantly put others down. It tends to affect us more as due to our sensitive nature we know how much words can burn, so we wouldn't want to inflict that on someone else and we cannot understand someone who does this so freely and easily as if it is a sport to them. It took me a long time to stop being angry at my mother for the things she said and did to me in my childhood. Why had she never once been proud of me? Why did she put me down all of the time? Why did she make me feel like a burden to her? I realised I would never get the answers to these questions, because my mother just isn't available on the same level that I am on. And you will find this with a lot of people. We think because they are 20 years plus older than us that they are going to be more evolved than us, but that is simply not true. You are very evolved because you are highly sensitive, but 90% of the planet are not. I realised all that anger I was carrying around was just weighing me down even more, so I chose to release it. I could have spent a lifetime being angry at my parents, but who made them the way they were to behave like that? And who made those people like that? And should I go back and be angry at them instead? My parents were frustrated and disappointed with the program they too had been forced to follow like so many others. So, I choose now to focus my attention on the things I can change instead of the things I cannot. The ideal situation would be that we only had good positive people around us all of the time, and a lot of gurus will tell you to rid toxic people from your life. And while I agree this is good advice sometimes, we can't always do this as these people may be people we are stuck working with, or family members, or long term friends that we simply aren't ready to let go of. So we have to learn to accept them the way they are, not try to change them and not let them take our energy. It's not your job to sort other people's problems out or make them a better person. It is **their** responsibility to do that. You can lead by example and support and advise them, but it needs to be them that does the hard work, and if they are not willing to do so and just want to play victim and pile all their shit on you, then walk away. We all know or have known the victim types; the ones that are bedridden and crying all over you one minute telling you their life is over and how nothing ever goes right for them, then the next minute they are full of beans and off on a fancy holiday or going out on a date with a new love interest. A good dynamic to read up on is the 'victim triangle'. A quick brief on it is that there are 3 positions to the victim triangle: the victim, the rescuer, and the persecutor. Unfortunately, there are a lot of people whose role is to be a victim their whole life. The emotional vamps I mentioned who just want to use you to moan at and tell you what a victim they are all of the time and how hard they have had it. When you try to fix their problems, they won't let you, they will have a reason why that won't work, and it just goes round and round. I have a friend like this who I used to spend a lot of time on trying to fix, to the point it left me physically and emotionally ill as she kept taking from me, never giving back and never acknowledging the time and energy I would give to her. So I would flit between the 2 roles of the victim triangle, of one minute being her 'rescuer,' trying everything I could to sort these never-ending problems out for her, to the next minute getting extremely frustrated and angry at her for moaning constantly and telling me my effort wasn't good enough! So I would then lose my shit and turn into the 'persecutor' and say some pretty cutting things to her. At the time I didn't realise that both roles 'equally' kept her in victim mode. When I took a step back and watched what was actually going on in her other relationships, I realised it was the same dynamics in those too. Her family were cruel to her, everyone around her was a bitch or a bastard, it was **always their** fault, never hers. I never saw it before, but suddenly I saw it plain as day. So I immediately removed myself from her victim triangle and lessened contact with her, and though we are still friends today I do not entertain her at all when she is in victim mode. I just nod nonchalantly and say "oh dear, that sounds pretty shit, what are you going to do about that then?" I remain completely separate from her and her emotions. Then if it carries on I just say "Ok this is getting a bit heavy for me mate, can we talk about something lighter as I've met up with you to have a nice time, and I'm not a trained counsellor you know?" Obviously, she doesn't like that very much as she is not able to be in victim mode and we are no longer close friends because of it, as the dynamics have changed. Sometimes she will try her best to get a raise out of me by being passive aggressive to try to get me to turn 'persecutor' but I stay completely aware of what is really going on when I am with her or talking to her so I am able to stay completely calm no matter what she says. It's a great shame she is like this as she has such a fun and interesting side to her that I really enjoy being around. But as I said before people are at different stages in their lives, and unfortunately some will never become self-aware, and you cannot and will not change a person who has chosen to be a victim all of their life. This is for them to change and take responsibility for. Now that I love myself, I no longer feel any pressure to help other people, including friends. And I no longer have the 'need' to fix others. Although I really like helping people (who want to be helped) and I get immense pleasure from it, the difference now is I 'want' to do it, I don't 'need' to do it. And I have no qualms in cutting my help off if it is being abused. If you are spending most of your life rescuing other people, stop and ask yourself why? Are you doing it because underneath you want someone to rescue you in the same way? Well if that is the case then I know someone who is perfect for the job (you!) Don't be afraid to lessen contact or cut off friends that are damaging to your mental health. It is very wrong of them to be treating you like this in the first place. There are plenty of people out there in the world who will cherish you for the wonderful friend that you are. So start opening yourself up to new opportunities where you can meet these people.

So, wrapping up on this chapter, you now have another essential tool for your kit 'gratitude.' I can't tell you how grateful I am for reaching that turning point 3 years ago where my world epically fell apart. And yes although it was proper brutal at the time, it forced me to take a completely different direction in life (I'll tell you more later on) where I had to invite new people and new experiences into my life, which in turn led me to have the courage to heal myself. It led me on to some wonderful adventures and fantastic people, and it showed me just how resourceful and capable I really was. I discovered the things I was really passionate about; writing and helping people. Which led me onto taking a course in life coaching, where I now help people online from all over the country with motivating them in all sorts of areas in their life. I absolutely love it. And I am writing all the time now too, there is no stopping me from it. Sometimes we can't imagine being happier in a life completely different to the one we currently have, and we can cling onto it, when really, it's time to let go of it. I couldn't imagine at that time that I could be happy again after splitting from 'the one.' But if I hadn't had split from him, I wouldn't have met my astonishingly awesome partner I am with today, who has helped me finally experience what a loving adult relationship really feels like. I've never met someone so supportive, considerate and acceptive of my feelings before. And the thought of not having met him makes my heart wince. It makes me feel really shaky, just the thought of not knowing him, not spending time with him, not having all our silly in jokes and cute names we've created for each other. I still to this day call him HNB (Hot New Boyfriend) in fact his number is still stored in my phone contacts as HNB. It is unimaginable to me now to think of all our memories we have built together being erased, and not just him either, as he also has a little boy who thinks I'm the best thing since sliced bread, and the feeling is mutual. (smiley face)

Before you go to sleep each night (while you are still conscious) think of 5 things to be grateful for that happened in the day. Then think of 3 things to congratulate yourself about.

Find a quiet time to listen to 5 mins of music that affects you on a deeper level and tell yourself you love yourself over and over.

During the day tell yourself (not out loud) that you love yourself over and over, just keep repeating it, 'I love myself, I love myself' every time you become mindful and think about it start saying it.

As you are dropping off to sleep at night start talking to your subconscious and tell it whatever you want it to hear. Maybe it's a habit you want to stop, maybe it's a problem that's hanging over your head that you need a positive outcome from, maybe you want it to give you some information the following day, or maybe you want to achieve a goal or dream. You decide. While you are still in that lingering state between awake and sleep visualise the things you want happening in the way you want them to. Remember for it to work you have to speak it, see it and feel it.

So that is where the rope leads to, my love. I can dangle it down to you by showing you what will truly heal you, but you have to do the work of pulling yourself up it by taking the actions and making the commitment to yourself to love yourself no matter what. You'll probably have to stop a few times on the way but hold strong and give yourself a good talking to, and then fiercely push on with the process like nothing else matters, because nothing else does matter.

Anxiety Matters

What is anxiety? There are so many different types of it nowadays aren't there? There's social anxiety, general anxiety, driving anxiety, anxiety of small spaces, anxiety of open spaces, anxiety of heights, anxiety of anxiety, the list goes on and on. But if you break it down, what is it? It's **fear**. And it doesn't actually matter what you're fearful of does it? It's the fear that is the feeling. It's the fear you have an issue with? I can remember at the height of my anxiety becoming scared of using public toilets, not because I had an issue with the unhygienic side to it, but because I was scared when I locked the door that I wouldn't be able to unlock it again. It would play out in my mind whilst sat on the toilet that when I would attempt to open it, it wouldn't budge, or perhaps part of the handle might malfunction and come off in my hand, so I'd be 'stuck' in there, probably with a full scale panic attack for company. I started to get it even being in saunas. I'd be sat there having a nice time with a partner or friends, laughing away with them sipping prosecco on a 'relaxing' spa weekend while all the time staring at the sauna door thinking 'it's definitely locked itself, yep definitely jammed, we're definitely stuck in here. What's going to happen to us then? Sweat to death probably.' Now when my mind became highly anxious in my 20's it didn't start with every type of anxiety straight away. The social anxiety started first, and although that was immensely crap, I was still happily driving on motorways and using public toilets. But because I didn't deal with the anxiety, partly because I didn't know what it was, as anxiety wasn't a word that was used much back then, I allowed the fear to spread, and eventually completely take over my mind and body. So, what started with a fear of social situations then led to fear of driving; first with motorways then with bigger roads, then residential roads, and then just sitting in my car outside my house. A sudden thought one day in a locked toilet that there was a tiny possibility that the lock might be jammed and that I could potentially be stuck in there for hours led to a phobia of using public toilets. If you have anxiety you will already know that an anxious mind will seek and play out the most ludicrous catastrophic scenario possible, going from 0 to 60 in 2 seconds. 0 being completely calm and 60 being homeless, penniless, dead or paralysed, and hated by everyone. Because I was watching and believing these recordings playing out in my head, being locked in a toilet became a genuine real-life fear for me. And then it led onto other situations. I couldn't even enjoy a simple pleasant walk in the country on my own, something I really enjoy doing. I would drive to the countryside to enjoy the peace and beauty there by taking a stroll, but less than a minute into the walk I would start thinking of the potential danger lurking around me. 'That car that just drove past, the man in it looked at me for way longer than a glance. I bet he's a rapist and a murderer! Shit I bet right at this moment he is turning his car around and is coming back to bundle me into his boot!' Which as you can imagine totally ruined my peaceful walk and put me off wanting to go on future walks because I didn't want to feel those levels of anxiety again. Once you start to understand that anxiety is caused by thoughts brought on by fear that are there to protect us from danger, you will see there is no real malice there, it just needs tweaking. A lot of my installed fears came from when I was a child and my highly stressed mother was always yelling at me to 'stop doing that or you'll hurt yourself, hold my hand when we cross the road because it is very dangerous, don't come into the kitchen while I'm cooking otherwise you'll get burnt or scalded.' I understand parents have to monitor their children's safety and teach them how to be cautious, but I think there needs to be a gentler way of doing this, especially when you have highly sensitive children, so you are not sending out stress signals to them and that they don't end up growing up spending their whole lives walking around on tiptoes convinced that danger is lurking around every single corner. My mind grew up with that fear of danger, and not just with what might happen to me if I'm not careful, but also with others. I saw how fearful my mother was of everyone and everything around her. She would shout and scream and hold on for dear life to the handle above the passenger door in my father's car when we were little as he manoeuvred around busy central London. She never learnt to drive herself because she was too scared of it. She never learnt to swim because she was too scared of it. She wouldn't walk over bridges or go up to high places. She wouldn't go into lifts or travel up escalators. She wouldn't even use a cash machine (and still won't to this day) because she was scared someone might attack her and take her money. I saw her anxious moments even in relaxed situations when we were visiting other people, sat in their living room chatting and drinking tea. She would sit there with her rosary beads hidden in her pocket clutching each bead and silently saying a prayer to keep herself calm. She would bite her nails constantly too. All of this imagery got stored into my subconscious, so when I got older and started to become aware of feeling anxious, I subconsciously mimicked her actions. 'Monkey see monkey do'. And it wasn't just her anxiety coping mechanisms I started mimicking either. I have a habit of using the silent treatment with partners when I am not happy with them. I can ignore them for days, even weeks if I want to. I will literally pretend they don't exist, and I'm very good at it. The creepy thing is I wasn't completely aware I was doing this until I became mindful in recent years, and realised I was following what my mother did. She would use the 'invisible' tactic to ignore us if we upset her, which was a lot. And remember the invisible man that lived in my grandma's back bedroom?   So hopefully that will be enough to show you just how susceptible our subconscious mind really is. And that if it can be trained to copy detrimental actions then it can also be trained to copy advantageous actions. It is a good thing that our mind is making us aware of any potential danger, but it isn't there to nanny our every move. Once you have an understanding that all your different anxieties are driven by one thing 'fear' then it is easier to tackle, as you are just dealing with one entity now. And what is driving that fear? I would have said mine was making a complete fool of myself in some way in public and feeling totally humiliated by it. But ultimately my fear was being scared I wouldn't be able to cope in an awkward or tricky situation. I didn't believe in myself that I could handle it just as well as the next person. Like the trapped toilet scenario, I'm sure has happened to many people and would it be the worst thing ever? The worst-case scenario would be I'd be stuck in there for a couple of hours while someone removed the door from its hinges. And if I had already been practising calming techniques on my body routinely then it wouldn't be a problem to keep cool. Tell yourself 'I am strong, I am capable' regularly. This is a very powerful affirmation. As I said it takes time to get your body to relax and stop having panic attacks, and you will experience setbacks, but you have to keep on going with it and believe what you are doing will work. That's when loving yourself starts to work for you, because you'll know it will be worth the effort. And you won't care about the setbacks because you are far more focused on reaching the goal of 'happiness' for yourself.

I do sometimes feel social anxiety sufferers do have a lot in common with the S.A.S. They are permanently in 'top secret stealth mode'. They are very adept at hiding it from others and excellent at evading social situations. They will instantly be able to come up with a million and one incredible excuses as to why they cannot attend that party or gathering. *By the way thankyou grandma for dying 5,248 times for me.* I feel like they literally go into battle every day, smearing on the camouflage mud so that they can blend into the background and remain unnoticed throughout the day. Having social anxiety basically feels like a wicked witch has cursed you. You are still physically fit and can go anywhere and do anything, but 'you can't go anywhere and do anything.' And people who don't have social anxiety just don't get it at all. They say stuff like "well don't take any notice of what some stranger thinks, just focus on what you're doing." They don't understand that **all** of our focus is on what other people around us are thinking about us, that's why it's called 'social anxiety.' *Duh!* Because people can't physically see the anxiety, they can't understand why it's such a problem. If we were sat in front of them with a broken leg in a cast, they wouldn't tell us to go cycling and just get on with it. So it's a very isolating disorder as it's not really understood and gets confused with shyness. It's so hard manoeuvring your way around this world when you have it. And it's even harder to make relationships and friendships. I remember one S.A. person I met up with opening up to me and telling me that he thought of himself as a hidden treasure waiting to be discovered, as he knew he had all these wonderful qualities inside that would make him a great friend or partner. He is probably right about that, and he is also probably still sat in the shadows waiting to be discovered. It's very sad but that's another annoying thing with social anxiety, you can end up missing out on so much in life, including making connections with people, as we hang back and wait for others to talk to us and let them do all the work. Which usually results in us getting that emotional vamp for a new best friend, as they have no issues in doing all the talking and are more than happy to let you sit in the shadows behind them making them feel superior. So, you need to start putting yourself out there and start getting used to rejection. Out of 100 people you meet there will probably only be about 5 you truly connect with, so you need to get out there and start sifting. The worst that can happen if you try and make friends with someone is that they will not respond to you. So what?

Just move on to the next person. Focus on the solution not the problem. Finding good friends or partners is far easier if you have a common interest to talk about and share together, so by taking up a new interest or hobby that you are really interested in or good at will automatically bring these people to you. The good thing about doing stuff you are genuinely interested in is it will help you to focus more easily on what you are doing rather than the people around you. I started to notice that when I was completely absorbed in doing something I enjoyed I completely forgot about the people around me for that moment. If you've been in a relationship where you've felt insecure and paranoid about losing them due to your low self-esteem, you will obsess about them when you are not with them 'what are they doing? Have they stopped liking me? Have they met someone better than me?' But have you noticed when you go and do your own thing with your friends or family how you don't obsess in the same way? Sometimes you won't even think about them, because you are preoccupied with something else. Well, it's the same as that.

Start getting your social confidence up in small ways. Aim to get eye contact with 5 people a day. This can be anywhere, walking down the street or in the supermarket. Keep your head held up so you are at other people's eye level as much as possible. Start looking at people's faces, noticing the different expressions they have. If they look at you and you engage in some eye contact, smile at them and see how they respond. Most will smile back but some will look away quickly. It can be fun, a bit like 'extreme people watching.' When we have anxiety life can seem profoundly serious for us most of the time, and we are scared of letting loose as we are so used to being wound up tight inside. But we need to let loose and have some fun.

As social anxiety sufferers we can tend to try and fit in with normal people who don't appear to have any anxiety because we see them as strong. But they are not strong because they don't have anxiety, you are strong because you do have anxiety. Please don't ignore 'you' and try to be like them when you have so much to offer the world with your highly sensitive nature. We need more people like you in the world, not less. There are a lot of unkind, messed up people out there with all sorts of issues and problems masquerading as 'normal people,' for God's sake don't let them make you feel inadequate in any way for having anxiety and **feeling** your way through life. I would choose to follow you over them any day of the week. I feel one of the biggest problems in our society today is this one-upmanship nonsense. You've been to Tenerife, well then they've been to Elevenerife. You've had cod and chips for dinner, well then they've had shark and chips for dinner. Or you tell them something you did recently, and they say "oh I would have done it this way." Well I honestly don't give a rat's arse what way 'you' would have done it, because you're not 'me' and you weren't even there so it doesn't actually matter does it? Why do we need to always do one better than someone else? We must be really unhappy in ourselves to behave like that? Look at all the nasty troll behaviour online. They take an almost sadistic pleasure in cutting someone else to pieces. That is not 'normal' behaviour, it's fucked up. People and their never-ending self-important opinions drive me mad. I wasted so much of my life worrying what these people thought about me, when really it probably should have been the other way around. People will **always** talk about you behind your back. It's not something you can change no matter how nice you are, because if someone is unhappy in themselves, they will always trash talk others.

Romantic relationships are always a problem for an anxiety sufferer too because there is so much emotional grey area involved. I always liked to think of myself as a lone wolf before, as I spent so much time on my own, and I could never trust other people not to hurt me. But I learnt more about myself from being in a connected relationship than I ever did from being on my own. Relationships teach you so much, and we can thrive as humans if we are in good ones. But for a relationship to work you have to be able to be vulnerable and get emotionally intimate with your partner, which is terrifying. I was in a relationship for 3 years in my late 20's where I never told him about any of my anxiety, not a single word in fact. I never even mentioned the word 'anxiety' to him. So, I know it's possible to be in a long-term relationship pretending the whole time to be someone else. But unless you reveal to them who you truly are, then you're never really going to have a relationship. With anxiety and low self-esteem, we tend to feel we are not good enough for someone, not attractive enough. A relationship is not based on how physically attractive you are. If that person was attracted to how you looked in the beginning then they will always find you attractive regardless of other more attractive people being around. There will always be attractive people around your love interest. That is something you will never change. A relationship is based on the bond the 2 of you have created 'together' and when you have this bond they could meet a 100 hotties on a night out but that will never even come close to the bond they have with you. So stop trying to be the only attractive person in your partner's life and instead work on the things that actually matter to them. Be there for them, be their best friend, listen to them, don't play silly little games to test them, don't obsess about their ex's; they are an ex for a good reason, and everyone has a past, get to know them on a deeper level than their previous partners by opening up yourself. Give them 100% of you when you are with them but equally when you are not with them give 100% of you to whatever you are doing instead. Relationships can be absolutely glorious, but never lose yourself in that relationship. Make sure you love yourself more than anyone else and give yourself time to yourself and your interests when you are in a relationship. You must remain a whole person in your own rights within the relationship and have your own hobbies, friends, goals, dreams etc, as you must not let another person be the main source of your happiness. Your happiness is **your** responsibility. And if you truly love someone you would never put that burden onto them. If you do your own thing outside of the relationship you will have much more to talk about when you are with them. They will respect you more, and you will sweat the small stuff less, instead of having petty arguments because you don't feel you are getting enough attention or appreciation from them. Because you will give that attention and appreciation to yourself. If you want a partner to be honest with you then you have to be understanding with them. If people are going to cheat, they will cheat regardless of you checking up on them. Loving yourself will enable you to recognise the 'avoidant' types, who ironically you will want to 'avoid' yourself because they have all sorts of issues, and are emotionally stunted, and will never commit to you properly and will always keep themselves hidden from you. And these are the types that usually cheat because they cannot handle a deeply connected relationship. 80% of people who use online dating sites are avoidants, because it allows them to hide and have a long running series of short-term partners. I know because I used to be one of those avoidants. I'd always have the same answer to the commonly asked question by potential suitors; "Why is someone like you still single?" I would always reply; "I've just never met the right person" which was bullshit. I met plenty of right people.

One thing that really helped me in my healing was understanding that an anxious mind is a restless one. It's like babysitting a child with ADHD. You need to keep it occupied by focusing on positive thoughts and dismissing negative ones. You need to stimulate it with fun and exciting tasks. And you also need to tire it out by taking time out to calm it down. Next time you are watching something on television **really** watch it. An anxious mind will tend to only half watch something and still have a zillion thoughts babbling on and on. So try doing this; watch it with **all** of your attention. Look at the whole screen in every shot and scene, take the focus off what they are saying and look around. What are they wearing? What earrings has she got on? What is on the table they are sat at? What colour is the hat on the clothes rack in the corner of the room? Doing this expands your attention and also gives you an insight into just how unmindful you are most of the time. You can try this technique in lots of other settings as well like when you are out in public. If you have anxiety you pretty much live in your head, so start venturing outside of it. Ignore the thinking and just watch, non-judging, just watch. You need to practise and show control in calming your mind regularly too. Otherwise when you really need it to be calm when you are actually in a potentially anxious situation (like the trapped toilet) you're never going to be able to achieve calmness, and it will just go out of control. So start routinely relaxing it. If you don't like meditating, then think of other ways to keep still. It works better if you come up with these ideas for yourself as you'll be more inclined to do them then, and this is about **you** so make it **you.** But for example, you could just pretend to be a statue for 5 mins, set a timer for 5 mins and just get into a position and just hold it. You can pretend you've been frozen in time by your arch nemesis, or that you've been turned into a famous statue like the statue of liberty. Whatever you want, have fun with it but just do it. Completely freeze your body and your mind. At first your mind will be like 'what the fuck is she/he doing?' but just wait, after a minute or so your mind will think 'ok I guess we're really frozen' and it will obey and follow your lead. You have to start taming that wild stallion conscious mind of yours first before you can start getting control of your subconscious mind. Another good exercise is doing something in slow motion. We don't realise just how fast anxiety is working inside us on a daily basis, so just slow it down. This will feel really weird at first, which will tell you just how fast an anxious mind actually operates. It really doesn't respond well to when you first start slowing it down. It will probably get niggly then angry. Herbal calming tablets are good for helping to relax the mind. You could try the slow-motion exercise. Just spend 10 mins doing everything in ultra-slow motion. Move your feet to walk in slow motion just to feel the difference and note how the mind at first starts racing with it wanting you to speed up, then notice it gradually settling down. Other ways to slow it down when you are out and about are, deliberately take your time walking around, let other people go in front of you, hold doors open for people, put yourself in a rushing situation and purposely take your time, go to the back of the queue and see that the world didn't cave in on you because you didn't rush.

Practise sitting in a relaxed position and see how this makes you feel. Even lay right back on your chair with your feet up and hands behind your head, notice how that position sends a signal to your brain that you are relaxed. Practising relaxation is vital, even more so when your life does take off. You have to take time out to chill, there is no getting away from that. I've seen it time and time again with talented artists who are incredibly creative but their mind is firing out stuff all of the time and even though that stuff is pretty fantastic they end up burning themselves out, as you need to set boundaries with yourself and plan relaxation time into your schedule. You'll need it. If you have anxiety you will have a very vivid imagination, so start utilising it to come up with ways to stimulate that brilliant mind of yours. I like to feel myself as fluid energy rather than a solid being as much as possible when I am walking around, so I feel lighter and freer in my body. Be mindful as much as possible. When you meditate just sit quietly and just observe your thoughts, don't engage with them or judge them, just observe and let them come and go. Another way of controlling your mind is by doing a countdown every day. You can do this any time of the day, just relax down and close your eyes and just count backwards 'slowly' from 100 to 0. See the numbers in your mind. For some reason I use red balloons as my numbers, but you pick whatever works for you. All you are doing is attempting to get from 100 to 0 smoothly in one go without stopping. Sounds easy? Ha-ha, well try it. This exercise will show you just how much your attention does waiver and how little control you do have of your conscious mind. But with practise you will eventually sail through it. This is why it's such a good exercise, as it really does train your mind to listen to you. Brain games are great for your mind too, there are plenty of brain training apps to try which will give your mind a workout. Anxiety and stress go hand in hand, creating a lot of explosive anger that needs calming. The most amazing thing for me was once I took control of my thoughts I no longer got stressed because I no longer let my anger run the show. Do you feel angry a lot? Does it tend to be your 'go to' response in most situations? Think about it, is anger the only emotion you are good at expressing?

Now a big thing you need to check if you have anxiety and/or depression is your physical health. I took all this for granted, being a slim person for all of my life I never had to watch what I ate, so I ate a lot of crap. And having had chronic anxiety for so long I've had the joy of having pretty much every physical symptom of stress and anxiety out there; chronic muscle aches, headaches, light headedness, dizziness, sinus problems, tight throat/lump in throat, reoccurring sore throat from a weak lymphatic system, IBS, insomnia, extreme fatigue. Firstly, how is your oral health? This is a big indicator of what is happening in the rest of your body. Do you see a dentist regularly? If not, you must, this is something you cannot mess around with. Gum disease affects 1 in 2 people and if left untreated the inflammation spreads to other parts of your body and can lead to major illness and disease. The majority of diseases in our bodies are caused by inflammation. So, make sure you are flossing and cleaning your teeth properly every day. I was gobsmacked at how many diseases in the body can come from having inflamed gums; such as diabetes, arthritis, neck/back pain and colitis to name just a few. Oil pulling every day is a highly effective daily detox of the body through your mouth and will help to heal your gums. I have tried numerous different fad detox's in my time, but this is one that **really** worked for me. And all you need is a tub of organic extra virgin coconut oil from the supermarket costing less than 5 quid. It was the first time in my life where I experienced a healing crisis. My whole body reacted from the detox process from that very first evening and lasted for 3 days. This is common if you have a lot of toxicity stored in your body from a sluggish lymphatic system, as it can create a negative reaction when it is suddenly released. It was pretty frightening at first as I didn't know what the hell was going on, as I never expected just swishing some oil around in my mouth for 20 mins then spitting it out afterwards would be capable of affecting my whole body, but I can assure you that it did. After the healing crisis finished, I started to feel 'really' good and my energy levels shot up. Another good detox to try is a parasite detox. You'll need one containing wormwood. Parasites are ingested so easily into our systems nowadays especially if you bite your nails or fingers, and don't wash your hands before you eat, and so many of us have them and never even realise, and blame our stomach bloating issues on food intolerances, and we carry on oblivious to them living inside us stealing all our nutrients, so no matter how healthy we try to eat we always feel fatigued. I'm not saying a parasite is the culprit for your anxiety and stomach issues but it's worth looking into. Celery juice in the mornings is also another effective way of healing your body. Different things work for different people, so it's about finding what works for you. Eat as much of a plant-based diet as you can, avoid processed and fried foods, and minimise alcohol. Snack on healthy foods like fruit, cheese, yoghurt, granola bars, cherry tomatoes, raw carrot and pepper sticks. Water, water, water. Get plenty of sleep; if you have trouble sleeping because you are a light sleeper, buy some flat sleep phones and play white noise through them all night. If you grind your teeth at night don't buy a mouth guard (which just covers up the problem) practise jaw relaxing exercises. Practise nose breathing throughout the day, there are some excellent nose breathing tutorials on YouTube. Learning to breathe properly will strengthen your lungs. A dry mouth is common with anxiety, which if left can lead to all sorts of illnesses and problems, so suck sugar free hard boiled sweets or chew sugar free gum throughout the day to get your saliva glands working and give your clenched jaw a much needed workout. Exercise at least 20 mins every day. Have regular massage therapies to look after yourself, there are so many to choose from, I enjoy a deep tissue one for when I'm knotted up, and an aromatherapy massage when I just want to relax and unwind. I also have regular Bowen therapy treatments, which are fantastic for repairing and realigning the whole body. Also make sure you are giving yourself a daily lymphatic drainage massage, as this causes havoc in our bodies and brains if it is not functioning properly. Most people with anxiety suffer with a stiff neck, due to not exercising enough because of lack of energy/motivation so your spine eventually becomes weak and your neck suffers. So, you need to start doing body weight training every day to strengthen your core and spine. This is really simple to do, you can do it from home, there are plenty of free videos on YouTube to follow. You can do a mix of cardio (which is good for breathing circulation and the heart muscles) and strength building (planks, squats, lunges, press ups, sit-ups) but make sure the largest part of your workout is strength building. Making your body strong will help you in all areas of your life. Your posture will get better, your immune system will get stronger, your neck will no longer be sore from being too weak to hold your head up. And you see so much progress really quickly with body strengthening, literally after 3 sessions, which is why it is so good for you to do as you will feel your whole body getting stronger every day. And it also creates a relationship between you and your body where you will be totally in tune with it, and you will know how far you can go with a workout. If you suffer from excessive sweating, get a concentrated maximum strength antiperspirant that you use twice a week (there are many good ones online.) Learning the different acupressure points on your body is also really beneficial when you have headaches, dizziness and pain that is related to anxiety. Again, this is available for free online, you don't need to sign up to do a course in it or pay for this information. All of these things I mention are so cheap and easily accessible to you. Companies on the internet will try and convince you that you need a magic pill to cure your problems, and what are the chances, but they have that exact magic pill. Just remember they don't know you; they couldn't care less about your wellbeing; they just want you to part with your money. Don't let other people force their ideas and creations on you. They are not super intelligent master minded experts; they are simply good at marketing. Trust in your own body and your own mind. Be in no doubt what you eat decides how you are going to function as a human. You are going to need energy to have that life you really want, and you need to get it through a healthy diet. I know this paragraph has been a bit preachy and boring and I'm sorry about that, but honestly there is literally no point in sorting out your mental health if your physical health is poor. You need your body to be in good working order too to obtain your life goals and dreams. Once you start loving yourself you will naturally start to move into a state of wanting better for yourself, so you will automatically gravitate towards a healthier lifestyle.

As I said in the first chapter the world in which we live in is shrinking. We are told what to do more than ever, therefore we think less and less. And so, we lose our freedom of thought trails. We can't even queue up independently and mindfully anymore. At most supermarkets they have queue busters who tell you which checkout is next available. Go to the bank or post office, that has a screen and a silly sing songy voice telling you which cashier is free next. We might think this is supportive as it makes our life easier, but in the long run it stops you using your instincts and working things out for yourself, and making occasional faux pas that you would expect to make along the way, and seeing them as part of the journey and not letting them become a fear. One of our biggest fears in today's society is the fear of doing something embarrassing or humiliating in public. And having all of our decisions made for us make us even more afraid of it happening. It breeds anxiety by leading us to believe we are not capable of making our own decisions anymore. We are stuck in that management system from birth. It starts with being told what to do by our parents, then being told what to learn and how to behave (stay in line) at school, then college, then university, then the workplace. We are not encouraged to think for ourselves, as that's not how a system works. The trouble is all the great ideas and new inventions come from thinking outside of the box. So, when you're stuck inside it your brain will never think for itself and start doing what it's supposed to do for you 'create.' And you're never going to stop feeling anxious living such a restricted life, afraid to step outside of the management system, not doing what your brain actually wants to do. I told you about my upbringing, how there was so much control from my mother and from the religion, which is yet another management system to follow and obey. I didn't know what it felt like to genuinely live until a couple of years ago when I started to take the steps away from the management system and started following the flow. A life coach once asked me "What if your anxiety is only there because you are not doing what you are supposed to be doing with your life?" I couldn't make sense of that back then, but her question always stayed with me. We need to start thinking for ourselves, and question everything, and have our **own** tools to hand to live our lives freely and successfully.

Do the countdown as you settle down at night. Carry on with your visualising, see what you want to happen in real life in your mind.

A wise man once said 'Living in the future is anxiety, living in the past is depression, and living in the present is a blessing'

The Great Depression

If we could bottle a cat's mindset, we would have an anti-depressant that actually worked! Cats really don't give a shit about anything and just live for the moment. I'm not saying cats can't get traumatised, I worked in an animal shelter for a while and sadly saw this to be the case. I'm saying they don't get depressed about what they don't have. And they don't get depressed that they are not good enough the way they are. I spent a lot of time cat socialising at the centre, and then I also did a lot of cat-sitting for their new owners while they went on holiday, so I used to spend a great deal of my time 'cat watching.' And that's when I started to realise that they have a very enviable mindset. They never felt bad about sleeping their lives away, even on a bright summers day when they should have been out making the most of their short lives, it never bothered them that they preferred staying inside in a dark corner sleeping. They never got FOMO that other mondaine moggies might be out basking in the sunshine having a jolly nice time. I found myself being in absolute awe of these fascinating creatures that lived completely in the present and were totally immune to depression. Because for me I had spent most of my life living in the past wishing I had done things differently and reliving hurtful memories over and over. Depression stalked me for a very long time. I'd occasionally manage to escape away from it for a few days or sometimes even weeks, but then it would always find me and follow me around like the grim reaper. It really did feel like a whole separate entity to me that wasn't actually part of me. And that's the thing, depression is actually all in the mind. We can choose what state of mind we want to be in. Have you noticed when you've been mega down but then something really funny will happen and it will completely distract you and you'll start laughing, or you'll talk to your friend about your problems and they will cheer you up sometimes quite easily in that moment. It's because your mind just follows what you show it. You could actually choose to be deliriously happy if a doctor told you that you had a terminal illness and only have weeks to live. It wouldn't be seen as the correct way to respond, but you could do it. We're conditioned to act and respond to situations in certain ways. 'Normal' ways. But what is normal? Is it just what the majority says is normal? Imagine right now if nobody ever had an opinion on anybody else. Would you still be depressed about your situation if nobody else thought it was crap or sad? Would you still want the things you want if nobody praised you for getting them or were envious of you being successful? It's a good thing to check in on the ego, as a lot of the time it's the ego that is telling us we 'should' have these things. You will know when you really want something regardless of what other people will think of you as it will burn into your soul. You will desire it, and you won't be able to function without working towards obtaining it. You will want to show yourself what you can do, not anyone else. How can someone else possibly know what you are capable of? They can't! So never focus on their opinions about it. Focus on the path that **you** choose to follow, and if Neggy Nagbag shows up along the way then take away the one power it has over you – your focus.

Mental health awareness has gotten so much better in the last few years with all the campaigns that have been running but we've still got a long way to go. There is still a stigma attached to poor mental health, that having it is a sign of weakness and that you are somehow inferior if you do have mental health problems. Well I can tell you right now you're not inferior, in fact you're the opposite! Having deep emotional feelings and knowing something is very wrong with the planet is not inferior, that is **awareness**. And humans that are aware have the ability to change the world.

The program creates so much unhappiness and depression for us all. School, college, university, gap year travelling abroad, career, meet the one around 25, get married late 20s, 2 kids in early 30s, have garage parties in your 40's. (That's a thing you know? People actually have parties in their garages for something different to do.) The sad fact is most people are so bloody institutionalised that they never really ever left school. For them it's still all about trying to get in with the popular clique, to be noticed, to be relevant. They think they are being original and unique in their choices, but they can't see they are totally brainwashed and that in fact there is nothing original or unique in what they say or do. They think they are remarkable by having a bucket list. I remember when bucket lists were trendy and so that was quite a popular question I got asked when I used to internet date; "What's on your bucket list?" Or "Where do you see yourself in 5 years?" *Well since you asked, I am suicidal so I will hopefully be dead by then. TMI?* Speaking of internet dating, or as I like to call it 'disposable dating' please avoid it, especially if you are either a hopeless romantic or have low self-esteem and suffer with depression. It is so forced and fake, you only know what they choose to tell you. As I said before the majority of people online are avoidants so they are just looking for a quick fix, and it can leave you feeling very desperate and empty from meeting so many people over a short period of time. You start to frantically search for common ground between you both to make it seem like you haven't completely wasted your time and that you 2 are indeed a fit "oh you like peanut butter too? This could be the start of something special then." Plus, you end up giving chances to people that you would normally run a mile from in the real world. It is far better to meet someone in a real-life situation either through friends or by doing a hobby you enjoy. You will have a far better understanding of who that person really is, and you will have a good solid base to work from. But going back to people and their boring fuck it bucket lists, most people don't have imaginations like us, so they find it easy to make decisions as they don't actually have many independent thoughts of their own, they just follow the shepherds. And I've found with them that they tend to be in professions that one of their parents or siblings were in before them. That's why you'll find a lot of people have breakdowns or a midlife crisis when they are older because they come to realise that they haven't actually done anything of what they really wanted to do. They kid themselves that drinking a bottle of wine every night at home is ok because they are still going to work every day and leading a normal full life, so the wine is a reward. You can see they are covering up big time, right? Which is why it is so important to start focusing on you and stop comparing yourself to these people. It is said that comparing yourself to others is the quickest route to misery. It's true, as you don't really know what you are comparing yourself to anyway, it's just a mirage that they are doing well for themselves. They haven't actually got a clue what they are doing. They are just winging it and sinking a bottle of wine every night hoping for the best.

There's so much pressure to know who you really are. I now know I don't want to know exactly who I am, as I'm not the finished product and I never will be, and that's liberating. The program is just an illusion, there are people all around the world following a completely different way of life and are perfectly happy. Think about people across the world who spend their whole lives in silent meditation or nuns living in convents for all of their lives. These people would be seen in our society as wasting their lives and not actually living, but they are living. There are so many alternative ways to live your life, so we need to break away from this one size fits all notion and find what works for us.

A good way to ease your depression is to understand your triggers for it. Some of mine are rejection, being ridiculed and feeling like a burden to someone. They all started in my childhood and got piled on with more of the same as an adult. I can remember when I was about 9 and was in Ireland on our Summer holidays and there were always a lot of kids living and visiting on our street, and we were all very friendly. My mother was so much more relaxed when she was back at her home in Ireland, so I had more freedom there and it was a time and place where everyone knew each other and nobody locked their doors and we would all wander in and out of each other's houses as we pleased. And one of the neighbours had a lovely bright green VW campervan that he would take all the kids out in for day trips, it was so much fun squeezing everyone into it. Then one day when I was playing in the street the campervan guy says to me "sorry TJ we have no room to take you with us today, so you will have to be left behind." I was the 'only' child that wasn't being taken out in the campervan. That memory will still sting right to this day if I let it as I can recall it like it happened yesterday. This grown arse man who had children himself, who supposedly understood children had feelings I'm guessing, told my 9 year old self 'you're the only one who isn't coming along, we don't want you, you're not as good as everyone else, so we're leaving you behind to play on your own while we fuck off on an adventure to the beach and have ice-cream and create unforgettable memories that we're all going to bang on about constantly when we finally return.' Fucking outrageous! So now when someone rejects me as an adult it instantly takes me right back to that exact time and place and I experience it all over again. My parents and siblings used to laugh and poke fun at me a lot as a child as I was the youngest, so I was always referred to as 'the stupid one' so even now I really have to speak calming words to myself when someone is poking fun at me so I don't have a complete meltdown. And I always felt like a burden and that I was in the way as a child, so again I can easily get triggered if someone looks at me in a way that makes me feel they are thinking these things too. Obviously, my family was always a big trigger for me. Just being around them even years later as an adult would send me into a depressive state for weeks after seeing them for only a couple of days. It was because I didn't love myself and I would let all the negativity from them and the past back in. Just because they are my family and are all older than me does not mean they are wiser than me, far from it. They say kids can be cruel, well so can adults! I've witnessed so many nasty comments from a parent to a child. I remember a family I did a few cat sits for who were absolutely lovely and invited me into their home with open arms, and I would stay the evening before with them if they had an early start the next day. So they would always cook me a nice meal and treat me like I was part of the family. One of the times we had had a great evening with some really interesting chats. The mother was this beautiful angelic looking being who always wore white and spoke with a velvety smooth soft voice, she had such a calming manner to her and was very spiritual and self-aware. The wine had been free flowing all evening and she started to talk about how important it is to think positively, which as you can imagine this chat was right up my alley. Then, out of the blue she turns to her 20 year old daughter and loudly proclaims "the opposite of you basically, because you are so negative and just attract loser men to you all the time and never have anything good going on in your life." I was mortified. This woman who I really respected and admired and found so interesting and talented was openly verbally abusing her own daughter! If you spoke like that to a stranger down the pub, you'd get a bloody good kicking, so why is it acceptable to get away with speaking to your child like that? Parents have no idea the devastating lasting damage they are doing to their children with their comments, especially if their children are highly sensitive. It showed me once again not to put people on pedestals, as they are far from perfect and have many flaws. So never worship anyone. Stop looking for that special leader out there to guide you, because they will be flawed too. Be your own leader and saviour and use that adoration on yourself.

You may have noticed I use humour a lot to get through life. (well I hope you notice) Humour is undoubtably one of the best things a human can have and share, and it's saved my life many a time. One of those times was when I was so low I phoned the Samaritans, as I didn't know where else to turn at that moment and I was scared of what I was going to do to myself as I couldn't switch off from the dark thoughts, I was desperate. The lady that answered my call had to be at least 90, and she kept asking me to repeat myself. She listened to a few things I had to say then told me "I think you need a good holiday dear" and then proceeded to tell me all about her cat. I burst out laughing there and then, as you literally couldn't make that shit up. That lovely lady didn't realise that she'd saved my life that evening just through making me laugh. I was laughing about it for weeks after. That's the thing humour is a much more powerful frequency than depression, so it will win every time. So remember that, and next time when you're really down watch or listen to something really funny. I believe the universe was sending me a message that night, telling me that it could hear me and cared about me on that phone call by providing me with 2 of my favourite things in the world; humour and cats. Speaking of cats; cat videos are great for making you laugh, as well as cartoons, comedians, humorous podcasts and audiobooks, classic comedy films as well as modern ones. There's so much to choose from. Force yourself to watch 5 hours of comedy if you have to, if you are in a bad state. I once read a story about a woman who was told she had a terminal illness and had weeks to live. She went home, turned her phone off so the doctor couldn't contact her and stayed in bed watching old comedy movies for a whole week and cured herself of her illness. Is that story true? I don't know but I'd like to think so, we already know how powerful the subconscious can be, and laughter is supposed to be the best medicine. We don't give humour enough credit in our lives today. A lot of the time it is seen as a negative thing to be laughing too much. I remember when I worked in an office back in my early 20's and we would get into big trouble for forwarding 'funnies' to other people's work email addresses. The 'funnies' as they called them were comedy clips and videos we would send to each other, mainly to make each other laugh, I never saw the problem. Are we not able to work if we have laughed too much that day? Heaven forbid.

It's all about finding ways to make yourself feel good when you suffer from depression. I'll let you into a little secret of mine. When I have a good thing happen to me now I like to visualise myself as I am now telling 25 year old me what just happened, and that things are going to be ok for them as they have all this good stuff coming. It may be because I have watched far too much sci-fi in my life, and I have a sneaky suspicion that we are actually on some sort of time loop, so I always send cool messages back in time just in case. And this thought of mine forces me to seek out good things to send back, because I haven't forgotten how bad that younger me felt. Music is also an immensely powerful mood lifter. If you are feeling down or a bit flat just stick your headphones on (as it's better loud and in stereo) and listen to some 'fun' music. There are plenty of great 'emotional' songs out there about losing love and being in turbulence, and while there is a time and a place for those sort of songs, they are not the songs you should be listening to when you're feeling down. You want fun silly songs that don't really make any sense to your analytical mind but just make you smile and feel that fun energy. I'm a huge 80's fan so I'm always going to choose songs from that era such as 'Prefab Sprout – King of Rock and Roll'. 'Timbuk 3 – The Future's So Bright I Gotta Wear Shades.' Or Huey Lewis and The News – Hip to Be Square. Find your happy songs and play them to yourself regularly to escape the seriousness trap of life. I also always write positive stuff down on the notepad in my phone so I can look at them if I'm ever feeling down or lacking motivation. It can be anything, it can be a nice comment someone has made about you, it can be something you have achieved, or something you feel positive about doing in the future. And once you start loving yourself there will be plenty of things that you will feel positive about doing in your future. And you're **never** too old to start these things. I worked for a hospice care charity for a while, and I remember in our training they made us do a practical test where we all had a piece of string and we had to cut off the life we had lived so far in stages and see what we felt we had left. I was the youngest volunteer there by at least 20 years but interestingly my end piece of string was the shortest. I just presumed life after 40 or 50 wasn't really life and you were just on your countdown to death. It really opened my eyes looking at the long pieces of string of the women that were in their 70's and 80's. They were loving life and were really grateful for everyday they lived. And they didn't see it ending anytime soon. They still had tons of dreams and goals. Someone there started playing tennis at the age of 80. Another woman started truck pulling in her 60's, she lost her husband so wanted to have something to focus on so decided to get fit, which started with her getting a personal trainer to leading to her somehow getting into truck pulling. There are so many other older people out there with similar stories, look up Mary Wesley. She was one of Britain's most successful novelists selling 3 million copies of her books, incredibly she didn't start writing until she was 71 years old! She wrote right up until she was 91. And how about Ernestine Shepherd; the 80-year-old professional bodybuilder? She never even started exercising until she was 56, and her love of exercise grew from there. That's the thing, your passions don't have to be life-long dreams, they can come about just from starting something else. I get that it's hard to get into anything when you're depressed. I sometimes went for days without showering back then, let alone exercising, let alone writing or doing anything I really wanted to do. I just wanted to stay in bed binge watching films and eating crisps and sweets.

But now I love the thought of getting out of bed and learning new things and pushing my body further than I did yesterday. My subconscious has changed my life for me. It definitely wasn't a conscious decision for me to stop binge watching films, or stop eating crisps and sweets, or minimise alcohol. But because I gave into loving myself I successfully trained my subconscious mind to love me back, so now it only craves things that are in line with loving my mind and my body, and it no longer craves the harmful, wasteful stuff as there is no longer any rewards from them. Eating healthily fulfils you in a way that eating rubbish can never do. So when you get into healthy eating you just won't crave sugar, salt or carbs because your body will be getting everything it needs and is full. (like it is supposed to be) Yes it's very unnerving at first learning new things and adopting a new lifestyle where the rewards aren't instantly pleasing like lying in bed watching films shutting everyone and everything out. You are going to be opening yourself up to all sorts of potential hassles by leaving your bed, but the more you do it the easier it becomes, and eventually it will become a way of life for you and the rewards you will receive will be bountiful.

So study your heroes, appreciate them for what they have achieved but don't worship them and do not believe that they are superhuman, because you can be like them too if you study them enough. It's never the most talented people that make it, it's the most determined people that make it. If you become determined you can make it too, but you have to be prepared for the knocks, and trust me there will be many many knocks if you do go down that path. If you watch inspirational videos you will see just how many knocks they have had, but they kept getting back up. We tend to only be shown the finished version of our heroes, we don't see the blood sweat and tears it took them to get there. So if you want that too then you have to get into that same mindset of when you fail (which you will) you get back up, then when you fail again, you get back up again, then when you fail again, you get back up again, then when you fail again, you get back up again. You don't stop. You never stop. Stopping is no longer an option for you.

Another delightfully easy way of getting out of depression mode is by helping other people. This can be done on a big scale such as volunteer work or on a much smaller scale (still the same value) as helping people in everyday life. Even just picking something off the floor and giving it to the person who dropped it can make their day. Holding doors open for people, giving them the correct change in the carpark, giving someone directions. There are 100's of ways. You could find so many people to help if you went out for the day with that intention in your mind.

You have the same value to the universe now as you did when you were born. And everyone else has this same value. So, you now have the same value as a newborn baby or as a tramp living on the street. We all are given life, so we are all equal in the eyes of the universe and that remains throughout your life. When you truly grasp that, it takes any pressure from yourself away and makes you not only appreciate yourself but also appreciate others just as they are. We're all following a different path for different reasons so stop looking at their path and give your full focus to your own path.

Look for 3 opportunities a day to help someone, they are all over the place if you look. Letting someone out of a difficult road. Giving someone some money for carpark or similar. Opening a door for someone. Telling someone the shoes they are trying on in the shop suit them. Picking something up for someone when they've dropped it on the floor. The opportunities are endless, you just have to look for them. Instead of being in anxious tunnel vision mode open your eyes and look around. Every time you do one of these helpful actions praise yourself. Start acknowledging every little positive thing that you achieve throughout your day so you can start to appreciate how amazing and capable you really are.

This may sound creepy, but I feel very connected to you right now at this very moment as I am writing. I don't know you, but I feel you. Yes, there is a time difference from me writing this and you reading it, but as I said before about me sending messages and energy back in time, I can also send them forward in time. Good energy doesn't disappear when it is put out into the universe. The energy is still the same, and it is here now for you to receive.

Private! Keep Out!

So, I guess you know by now if you are highly sensitive you are also an empath, and probably a bit clairvoyant, but the other thing you probably are is 'introverted.' Understanding the introvert mindset is crucial for navigating your way around life on Earth as an introvert. I grew up thinking I was weird and peculiar because I acted differently to most people around me. My life would have been a lot easier if I had been aware of highly sensitive people and introverts. We like our own space, and lots of it. We are very choosy who we tell our secrets to. Small talk makes our skin crawl. We'd rather be asked 'when was the last time you cried?' than 'what have you got planned for the weekend?' We prefer one on one to groups, and we like to go deep with that one on one and understand what makes them tick and we want them to tell us everything about themselves. But we're not too keen on giving away too much about our inner selves, are we? (winking face) We love psychology and can spend hours people watching. We love to analyse stuff and we never make rash decisions, though it may seem like that to others as we don't tell them what we have been planning in our heads for ages, so we usually just spring it on them when we are set to go. We tend to be incredibly creative and can recall an extraordinary amount of details and conversations we have had from many years previously. 'Research' is our favourite pastime. *Alright obsession then.* We are methodical and scientific thinkers and we want things to be done right, so much so we can get obsessed with projects, which is why we prefer working on our own. The 'space' thing tends to be an issue for others in our lives as they don't get why we need so much of it, and why we don't want to be spending time with them or other people having 'the fun' but we don't just like our own space, we actually **need** it. Because of all the deep emotions we have, and because we take in so much of other people when we are with them, we need time to recharge afterwards. When I was younger, I would need 5 days of recharging after just 1 night of socialising. When I was working in an office environment full-time I was more than happy to spend every weekend completely on my own if I could get away with it, as I had more than enough interaction time at work during the week. My work colleagues never got it, they'd want to know what I got up to at the weekend, and most of the time I'd have to lie or be vague to get them off my back. When choosing a romantic partner, I always made sure they had something else going on in their lives so I would get plenty of space from them. So they either worked away a lot, or were workaholics, or were surgically attached to their family. Now that I am more in control of my mind I don't need as much recharge time as I did before. I'm a lot more in control of not letting myself get completely drained with other people in the first place now. We are great 'active' listeners, it's like a superpower to us. People love to tell us stuff, so we need to be careful they are not negative people dumping their neggy energy all over us. People have told me when they are with me it feels like they are the only person on the planet because I give them my laser focus. I remember on the majority of the internet dates I went on the guy was more than happy to bang on about himself for the whole date, so by the end of it I knew all about his job, where he lived, where he grew up, his family, what his dog had for lunch that day, but he wouldn't have been able to tell you a single thing about me. We are comfortable being the one 'that listens.' I used to struggle with social interactions big time as a kid. When I went into a room with lots of extended family members all sat down conversing together, I would go and sit behind the sofa, which you can't really get away with as an adult. *A Murray could probably get away with it!* I just couldn't cope with all the different energies in the room and questions fired from different angles, it was too difficult for me to steer. We like to know the who, what and where of every social situation we are going into because we hate surprises. I eventually managed to master the art of small talk from observing and mimicking people I felt were good at it. And yeah sometimes I still have those awkward moments now when you suddenly think 'are we having too much eye contact right now, or am I sounding boring?' but then I just see how amusing the situation is for both of us and laugh to myself. As introverts we also hate people creeping up on us, and we can't tolerate loud sudden noises. I remember once a friend taking me to a 'sound journey.' I thought this was something I would enjoy as there wasn't supposed to be any audience interaction, and you just had to lay down on a mat with a duvet wrapped around you and listen to the sounds. I think if it had been gentle instruments like angel bells or the harp, I would have enjoyed it, but it was very harsh instruments like the gong and the didgeridoo. I hated every minute of it! It actually felt like I was being physically assaulted, and it made me feel unsettled for a few days afterwards too, and to make it worse the facilitator wanted to have a group discussion after each piece. *What did I think of that last piece you played? Well it made me feel like I was being slowly tortured to death in a dark hole. Thank you so much!* I was out of there at the first toilet break! Never feel bad if something doesn't feel right for you, trust your gut and just get the hell out of there! I used to feel weak for running away from so many situations and I wondered how our kind managed to survive so many generations, why weren't we killed off in early evolution? As back then only the strongest survived to go on to reproduce. I read some interesting material about it and it seems we were one of the strongest! Think back to caveman days *get ready for a cerebral lowdown guys* when we were looking around outside of our cave to check it was safe for us to venture out. There's a giant bear in the distance that we don't want to mess with. We can tell we have time to run past without it noticing us, but as the introvert we stop and reassess that it is indeed safe, when we notice a venomous snake just outside of our cave, and if we hadn't double checked for danger we would have stepped right on it and died. The extrovert caveman in this same scenario just sees the bear and thinks 'yeah I can make it' so Mr. Cocky gets instantly killed by Mr. Snakey. I spent so much of my life wanting to be an extrovert and be loud and fun with a memorable personality. I felt like I didn't actually have a personality, and I just seemed to fit around or morph into who I was spending time with. I have a few extrovert friends who really are a lot of fun and have given me so many stories to tell from our crazy hedonistic adventures together. But extroverts aren't Gods, even though they can sometimes seem this way to us. They can actually be quite annoying after a while with all that 'full on' energy, and they never really listen to you, and can be incredibly insensitive and are usually surface people with 'cocktail eyes.' Which basically refers to when you are talking to someone at a social occasion one on one, as we like to do, and they are just saying 'mmm hmm' a lot to us while they keep their glass up to their face sipping their cocktail whilst they sneakily look around for someone more interesting or more relevant to talk to. They are the opposite of us. They love being in groups of people and they get recharged from being in social situations, and spending time alone drains them. It can be difficult for introverts as life does seem swayed towards to the extrovert. It's seen as healthy to work as part of a team and do group sports and go to endless social events at the weekend. Sitting at home alone on a Saturday night reading a book or watching a movie in your onesie is seen as dull and unhealthy. But we need to start profiting from our introvert traits and skills and see just how brilliant we are as humans. Take advantage of the fact that you can spend so much time alone and are able to organise and motivate yourself without needing others to help you. Start working on some personal projects. Your creation could be a product, service, business, novel, script, painting, song lyrics. All the best inventors and creators were and are introverts; Albert Einstein, Steven Spielberg, J.K. Rowling, Bill Gates, Mark Zuckerberg and Elon Musk are just a few. Look at what they've achieved with their introverted minds. They wouldn't have had these ideas and made them happen if they were extroverts. People tend to listen to the loudest person at the table, but most of the time they are the worst choice as they just blurt out the first thing that comes into their head. There are so many problems further down the road following cocky big mouths who can talk the talk but can't actually walk the walk. I have a couple of friends that if I had to stick a label onto them it would read 'pain in the arse.' They are extremely vocal about everything, and I hate going to restaurants with them as they ask the waiter every question under the sun and seem to complain to the staff about 50 times while we are there. But there is no doubt this attitude gets them what they want. I don't know whether it's because people just think 'for God's sake just have it so you stop going on at me' or whether because of their confident manner they come across more deserving so tend to get what they want; pay raises, money off expensive purchases, better deals, free stuff. Although I certainly would not like to act like them all of the time as it comes across unnecessarily rude and stressful for both parties, I have been able to mimic them in certain situations when I have been badly treated by a company or establishment, and it really has paid off big time. I've been stunned at how being assertive, standing my ground and not taking no for an answer has miraculously turned around situations for me in my favour that otherwise would have cost me a lot of money, hassle and stress. So it is also a good idea to watch some training videos on becoming more assertive. Standing up for yourself is not the same as being a bully, and it will benefit your communication greatly with others if you are not afraid to speak your truth, again this will come fairly easy to you once you start loving yourself. Also spend time watching programs and videos online about successful introverts because you will be able to relate to them so easily and you will start to see and feel that you can do it too. I've watched a lot of J.K Rowling interviews because I feel I can really relate to her, and also because she is such a humble modest woman which makes her so likable. I am in no doubt she is also highly sensitive as well as introverted from the things she talks about. And what I like about her the most is that she is very open about her insecurities and anxieties, and that although the money has given her a more comfortable life, it really isn't about the money for her. She gets pleasure from sharing her gifts and helping so many people across the globe. It could be interesting for you to find out where your introversion comes from, as there is usually someone in your extended family that you take after. My father's mother, which should be my gran right? No, this is my family we are talking about remember? I was told she was my eccentric great aunt because after my father came to England he reconnected with his mother but again my mother worried about the shame this might bring, so they told everyone she was my father's aunt. My mother always made snide comments to me growing up about how she thought I took after my 'contrary and strange' Aunty Jean. I feel sad I never found out she was my actual grandma until after she had died. But I cherish the memories of us visiting her every month on a Friday night in her tiny flat in East London where the graffitied lift was permanently broken, and we would have to climb what seemed like 3,000 huge freezing cold concrete steps to her flat on the top floor of the high rise building. She chain-smoked and drank whiskey and didn't give a damn. She would tell my mother to shush when she started getting on her nerves (which was often) and she never once had a problem telling us all to leave at the end of each visit when she had decided she had had enough of us.

Start watching inspirational videos of famous introverts you admire. Tune into yourself and your exceptional gifts that you haven't yet uncovered. Do something creative each day; draw, write, sing, dance, invent new ideas. Your creations don't have to be perfect or mean anything, you are just experimenting for now.

Realise just how special and essential to the world you are for being an introvert. Use that mimicking ability to your advantage by spending time with people who are successful and happy in their lives. Find where you want to head in life, and start following the flow.

Follow The Flow

You have probably heard the term 'go with the flow,' well I am introducing another term to you; 'follow the flow' which basically means instead of casually going along with what others want you to do, you actively pursue where your own personal flow is taking you, without questioning or judging it, and you remain open and curious to everything along the way. To me it simply means listening to your gut rather than your head, and letting the universe guide you on a journey of discovery by linking you from one situation to another. Life doesn't have to be predictable or the same way as it is for the majority. You can do things nobody that you know in your life has ever done or even known about. You just have to let it unravel naturally for you without too much thought or planning. You are following the natural flow of the universe instead of the tired old predictable contrived program you are forced to follow from birth. You start off with something simple and you let it unfold. When I found myself at rock bottom around 3 years ago, I had no choice but to move forwards as there was no more reverse space left for me. It suddenly made life remarkably simple for me; I needed somewhere to live and fast. So I looked up some rooms for rent online. I couldn't believe the very first one that came up in my area of choice search which was basically a mansion, advertising a room for rent. Some people would probably have thought it was a joke or maybe be daunted by it, or just plain put off with it being completely cut off and out in the middle of nowhere. But I knew when I saw it that was where I was going to be living. I couldn't explain it at the time, but it felt to me that the room had become available at the exact time I was made homeless, for me. It wasn't a rational thought in my head, it was an overwhelming feeling; a gut instinct, and the instinct seemed to override my conscious thoughts. I moved into my room in that mansion 2 weeks later. From that moment onwards I decided I liked my instinct far more than Neggy Nagbag (who never brought anything nice to me). I had been so worried the weeks leading up to this inevitable change that my life was over and that there was nothing good out there for me anymore. Yet by belief in something that sounded impossible but **felt** possible I completely changed my life. I went from being homeless and completely alone, to living in an idyllic country manor with an older couple; John and Laura, and their 6 cats. *What about the ghost?* They were an extremely wealthy couple who both worked away a lot of the time and wanted someone trustworthy and easy going around the place to keep an eye on things and look after the cats. I had never experienced relaxation and extravagance at this level in my life before. And the way John and Laura welcomed me into their home and lives with open arms allowed me to feel completely at ease and comfortable there. I slotted right in, like I seemed to in most places. They were so different from anyone I'd spent time with before, and the complete opposite of my own parents who constantly worried about every little thing and never took any risks in life. The rent of the room was also ridiculously low and included all bills and use of everything there including; hot tub, games room, gym, extensive gardens, weekly cleaner. I no longer had any pressure on me financially or emotionally so I could finally pause, take a breath and look around at the event we call 'life'. I had gone from living in an unbearable nightmare where I had convinced myself I was trapped inside it, to starring in a real life enchanted fairy-tale. Living with John and Laura meant I was able to observe them closely too. I wanted to know everything about them and what gave them that energy and relentless drive to succeed, which they both clearly had. They both came from working class backgrounds, so the wealth and success hadn't been handed down to either of them, so success definitely wasn't hereditary. Because of their grass roots they were very down to earth and openly displayed their flaws to me, so I really liked both of them instantly, and on a very deep level as time went on. Laura was actually the menopausal crash test dummy I mentioned to you in a previous chapter. There was strong mutual respect between us from very early on, which surprised me at first. As there I was living in their house as the '30 something- has gone very wrong with me' with just about enough stuff to fill my enormous room there but nothing else to show them, but that didn't seem to matter, they respected and admired me for the way I was as a person. What I had or hadn't achieved wasn't important to them, it was about how they felt when they were in my company, which luckily they felt pretty good as I would always listen intently to everything they told me. And I loved hearing all their stories and never got bored even when they were repeated to me several times. And I was also happy to let them rant off to me after a bad day, or moan about the other one to me, and they enjoyed me cheering them up with my candid nature and childlike silliness. I realised then how important and useful my gift of listening was, and how all the stuff I had endured previously where I felt I had been cursed, had all added to my gift by allowing me to be able to be truly empathetic, non-judgemental and understanding of another person's personal experience. There was no pretence between us either. We were completely authentic with one another, something I had never felt growing up with my family. We would watch shit tv together, poke fun at one another, go to the local pub and go out on bike rides together. After a short while I began to question myself. We got on so well and seemed actually very similar in a lot of ways apart from that one thing; that they were successful in their lives and I wasn't. It made me start to think that maybe it wasn't a case of The Murrays being better than me, as John and Laura certainly were not better than me, they had many flaws and faults that they weren't ashamed for me to see. The thought occurred to me that maybe I had just missed some important memo along the way, that success and happiness was an option available for me too if I wanted it. Ok so I had missed that one but maybe all I had to do was learn from someone who knew how to do it instead. I could learn from John and Laura. So that's what I did. From studying them in our time together through observation and quizzing, I found that the 2 definitive traits they both had that I did not were determination and strong belief in themselves. Many many problems arose for them while I was living there, but instead of taking them personally or burying their heads in the sand like I would have done they faced them straightaway and head on and erased every single problem and roadblock they encountered. Their problems didn't go away because they had magical powers or genius brains, they went away because they stood up to them. When I first started living with them, I branded them 'workaholics' and really didn't get the insatiable overdrive of energy they both had for work, as I didn't see the point of it. It seemed like a lot of hard work. Why didn't they just want to sit back and enjoy their life and money? But I started to see it was about more than money to them. It was about the passion they felt for making plans and goals in their lives, and they didn't want to stop anytime soon, so just as one mission was complete, they were straight onto the next pursuit, it **never** stopped. And it turns out 'passion' is infectious! Yes, that's right, if you spend enough time with someone who is truly passionate it will rub off on you too. So, I started to feel I wanted that too. I wanted that feeling of accomplishment of going after dreams and goals and making things happen for myself. They showed me that I could be the sort of person that would enjoy and flourish in that arena too. The passion seed had been planted in me....

About a week after moving into the Moggy Mansion I drove to the nearest supermarket and I noticed an animal shelter about 10 minutes down the road. Again, something inside me stirred, it was the 'instinctual shout out' again, and because it sorted me out so well the first time, I listened to it, I didn't question it at all. I drove straight in there and asked if they needed any volunteers. After a few forms were filled in and a few checks were carried out I started volunteering there one day a week. I'd always been a huge animal lover and extremely drawn to the feline variety which meant it was inevitable I would help look after the cats there. After feeding them and cleaning their enclosures I would socialise them and let them out one at a time to have some free roaming and playtime in the room and hallway. If a cat wasn't allowed out, I would go and sit in their enclosure with them instead, and I could happily spend a good hour just sat in there with them. One cat who had FIV (aids) would love coming to sit on my lap while I was in his enclosure and have me stroke him for the entire time. At first I had thought I was doing this work for the cats, but I learned that I was also getting a lot out of it too. It was so meditative for me. Being able to have those few hours to myself with nobody else around and no television, radio, internet or any other distractions. It was so quiet there doing my cleaning and then enjoying my time with the cats and connecting with them. I realised when I was there I was completely calm and present, and in the moment, just like the cats. Nothing else existed or mattered while I was there. My subconscious started to acknowledge that this was important to me and that I wanted more of this please. The next steppingstone was cat-sitting for the new owners of one of my favourite cats from the shelter. Which again when I was asked if I would do it I simply said yes as I knew then I was on my own yellow brick road and there was a flow to it, and I was going to follow that flow. That brief encounter of being asked to cat sit for one cat eventually led me onto travelling the world doing pet-sitting for all sorts of people in all sorts of places with all sorts of animals. As you can imagine my confidence skyrocketed from doing this job and going to all these new places and having to meet so many different types of people who put their compete trust in me, and basically thought I was 'The Cat's Whiskers' for looking after their fur babies so well. It was also so good for my mind being in new houses as I would have to be mindful all the time. Even making a cup of tea took focus, as everything was new and unknown to me there, so I had to think about where everything was and how it worked all of the time. It really helped a lot with my 'numbering' OCD too, which would completely take over my daily life and stress me out if I didn't do all of the numbered routines in order. Most of us are so stuck in our daily repetitive routines that we do them all on auto pilot, so we are rarely mindful with anything. Which is why it is so good for us to change things up, even in a simple way like switching the order we do our morning routine in, or taking a different route to work, or doing 5 mins of meditation in the morning to connect to and acknowledge our inner selves. With the pet-sitting I also felt really good about myself because the people I worked for respected me so much and they would write me some amazing references. It made me feel proud of myself because the things they wrote were not made up, they were all true. I started to see my own wonderful characteristics that other people liked about me, and how I made them feel so comfortable around me by listening to them and being authentic and open with them. I started to ask myself why had I spent so long abusing myself and choosing only to have people around me who would put me down or just want to make it all about them as if I was totally invisible? It was in that moment I chose to start loving myself.

I worked for some very wealthy and successful people when I was pet-sitting, so I stayed in some very lavish houses. But what I also noticed was it didn't matter how fancy the place was, they still had very out of date stuff in the fridge, messy cupboards and drawers, and some sort of quirk with their shower that they had to explain in great detail to me. It was like with John and Laura, although they were accomplished, they were still like everyone else underneath. They weren't born to be successful with special superhuman incites or powers. Also being left to my own devices in somewhere unknown to me showed me that there wasn't anything to stress about, because when problems came up, I sorted them out. All of these new experiences plus being out of a routine and away from the program stirred my creativity up again, and 2 things came to me; I felt like I wanted to write again, and I felt like I wanted to help people. I knew from my experiences that I was good at listening to people and cheering them up and motivating them. And mixing this with my fascination with human psychology and with what made people tick I took a course in life coaching, and then set up my own online coaching sessions where I could easily connect to people from all over the country. I realised that I didn't need to do it in the way 'they' tell us to do it, by having a boring stuffy formal office for them to sit uncomfortably in, they could do it from the comfort of their own homes instead, even their own beds in some cases where they were at rock bottom with motivation. When I started writing again the idea of this book came to me. At first I tried to ignore it, as a self- help book had never been something I had wanted to write before. I had a million fictional ideas and characters in my head and writing was usually an escapism for me, so the thought of writing something real and factual and potentially really dull didn't entice me one bit. Plus, I'd read a lot of self- help books and I always thought of the writers as being highly intelligent and inciteful. There would be no way I could match up to them. But the idea wouldn't go away, in fact it started to hound me and block all my other ideas, so I gave in and thought I'd at least try it. At first it was difficult knowing how I was going to lay it all out and get a rhythm to it, but then it suddenly just started to flow, and the creative side of me was flourishing with it, just as much as it did writing fiction. Also, writing this book made me see myself and my past in a way that no amount of soul searching, or therapy could ever have done. It was immensely painful acknowledging, revisiting and reliving memories from my past, but it also brought me some fantastic realizations about myself. It was so strange, I'd spent so long hiding myself from others, yet here I was laying my heart and soul bare to the world, and it was the most natural and liberating feeling in the whole wide world to me.

Because I liked following the flow so much after I moved in with John and Laura, I decided to take it a step further in my anxiety ridden social life where I chose to become a 'yes man' and say yes to any social events that were offered to me. From doing this the first social event I went to was a music festival, which I'd never experienced before, and I met a girl there who was into climbing. She asked me if I would like to go indoor climbing with her, 'yes' I said. I had never even thought about climbing before, and if I had thought about it too much I probably would have freaked myself out about it and make an excuse to get out of it. When I got there I had an induction and I was straight up the wall. Knowing that I was saying yes to anything social kind of turned it into an experiment for me, so I didn't stop and analyse the risks as I knew I would be doing it anyway, so what was the point in worrying about it? I needed to be strong and positive to get the best result from whatever I had said yes to. From going indoor climbing a couple of times I met a guy 'Max' who I clicked with straightaway, and he asked me if I'd like to go outdoor climbing with him. 'Yes' I replied casually. Now I didn't really understand what was involved in this. I'd only been on a climbing wall a few times so I didn't even twig that there would be abseiling involved. *Ffs.* Now the old me would have googled everything about outdoor climbing before going and thought 'Hell no.' But I didn't Google it, I just went. I still feel elated about it when I think about it right now. I abseiled, me, I abseiled. And not just once but 3 times in that day. Yes, the first time took a good 20 minutes for me to step off the edge backwards with a lot of coaxing from Max, and then suddenly something clicked in my brain and I just did it! And I absolutely loved it! So much so that I couldn't wait to climb back up and do it again! Man, when I reached the bottom and I realised what I had just achieved I was ecstatic, and the very first person I told was my 25-year-old self. I just knew she'd be pumped. I did it. No matter what else would happen in my life after that day, I had slapped fear around the face and abseiled down a cliff. Max invited me to several other social activities after that that I said yes to, including shooting guns at his gun club, archery lessons and sailing. The fourth 'yes' was to a boat cruise, *aka booze cruise* he had organised for his work colleagues. Now normally I would have stopped and thought 'I don't work with these people, so I don't know any of them, so why am I going? I'm going to be out of place and feel like an idiot.' But I had made that commitment to myself so I didn't think those things as what would have been the point as I had already decided that I was going. So, there I was stood at the bar on the boat on my own at 11am ready for the 11.15am set off. My phone bleeped about 5 mins later. It was bloody Max messaging me saying that he had to cancel due to illness but to have a good time without him. 'Brilliant! Thanks a fucking bunch Max.' So I was on a friggin 4-hour boat cruise with not one single person I knew on it and it was too late to get off it. Up until this point the 'yes man' thing had been working really well for me, maybe it had run its course. As I was looking at my phone in disbelief willing him to send me another message saying it was a joke and that he was still coming, I heard a male voice from behind me speaking softly; "hello are you Max's friend Tara?" I turned to face HNB. Man, when I locked into his eyes, I swear I felt a bolt of lightning go straight through me. "Erm yes, yes I am" I managed to spit out. He smiled that infectious grin I've grown so fond of and replied "well I work with Max and he asked me to look after you for the day as he's sick." I was suddenly not so unhappy and pissed off with Max for being sick. 'Thanks a bunch Max.' I spent the next 17 hours with HNB; 4 hours on the boat then we all tumbled off and went into the town and carried on the party. It was like something out of one of those far-fetched romcoms. Everything flowed so effortlessly and easily with him right from that first day to today. I never had to question what was going to happen next because I just knew it was going to go in a good direction, and it did. I would never have met HNB if I hadn't been a yes man and took risks and followed the flow. You too will be surprised what will come your way when you surrender to this way of living.

Living this way will also bring lots of synchronicities into your life, as you will never be so connected with the universe as you are when you are following the flow. And the universe will speak back to you with these synchronicities to show you that it is listening to you. When I had the idea for a self- help book all I met for about a month after that was authors. The following 2 housesits I did after I decided I wanted to write the book were both authors. One of those housesits had a cool café in a park that the pet owners recommended to me, so obviously I went to it with the dogs. And while I was sat there taking in the busy yet relaxed vibe of the place, an old guy in a mobility scooter who was also taking it all in started to talk to me, and what do you know he was an author too! We chatted and we laughed, and he told me how important humour was in writing. I'd never really thought about that before, but I felt like he was almost giving me permission to use humour in my writing. That's the thing once you start asking the universe for something it will listen and respond. And you will realise you are a creator of your own life.

Some cool things to read up on are 'confirmation bias' which is the tendency to search for information that confirms your beliefs. Or the 'reticular activating system' (ras); the part of your brain that filters out unnecessary information so that only the important information to you gets through. It's like when my friend got a smart car and was telling me all about it for hours, and for the next week I saw millions of smart cars everywhere. Now they were always going to be driving around but had my friend not talked to me about them I would never have noticed them as the 'ras' would have filtered it straight down the rubbish chute of my brain. Another example: because I got into watching 100's of motivational videos, my brain would seek out positive motivational stories for me wherever I was that kept me feeling good. So, you see we can start using these systems to tune into and focus on things that are going to help us in our lives. Like me with the motivational videos, I will now instantly spot a feel-good inspirational story, I am drawn to it because my subconscious believes this is important to me. For example; now if I am reading any news online, I will instantly spot a feel good inspirational story on there. I am attracted to it because I have watched so many my brain now believes this to be something important to me. Can you also see how destructive this system could be if you are only hearing and watching negative info all day long?

Don't be scared to have variation in life. People say you only have one life to live so live it well. Well I say we can have multiple lives within this one. Find the things that resonate with you and wake you up out of trance state. Accept you will default to autopilot at first for a while and be patient with your transition. Just keep getting back up and getting on with it again. It doesn't matter how many times you fail as long as you don't give up.

Pushing yourself will ultimately lead you into direct competition with others. Introverts tend to be intimidated by competition and see competitors as threats, which is the total opposite experience to extroverts. Extroverts actually enjoy competition and see competitors as friends. Competition is healthy, it's fun. It makes us try harder. You'll want to do better for yourself too. You'll want to get out there and start smashing those goals and giving yourself a big pat on the back. You will want to prove to yourself you can achieve things, as that's where the true value comes from. Yes it feels good when people admire us and are impressed by us but that's not enough. That doesn't give us the deep feelings of fulfilment and gratitude for being us. That only comes from inside ourselves, so we need to be working for our inner selves and making them happy. And that's the thing, it's not just creating all these wonderful things, it's also being aware of it every moment, that it is happening and realising that is what we are meant to be doing, and trusting in our abilities to create.

I recommend trying anything 'other worldly' to break you away from the everyday repetitive predictable routine of the program. Visit a psychic or have your tarot read, try to see one that has been recommended by someone you know. You don't need to visit one more than once a year if you find you enjoy it, as otherwise this is a waste of money as you need time to put into place what you have been told. They tend to be extremely positive with what they tell you, and it will plant a seed in your subconscious that you will believe is true, so you will make it come true. I was stunned at how many successful people I met that visit psychics. I personally believe the messages the psychics get are coming from our higher selves anyway, so it's basically tuning into ourselves. When I first visited a psychic, she kept referring to my future as 'the next chapter.' I don't know why (because I'd never met this girl before) but she just didn't strike me as someone who would say 'next chapter' and to me it was confirmation that writing was what I was meant to be doing. She then told me that she could see me healing lots of people in the future, then she looked rather puzzled and said "but I don't see you physically touching these people." Well, you know what I knew I had to write about after that! Now is that just me seeing what I want to see in it? Maybe, but so what if it is if it brings about positive reinforcement in my dreams? HNB's grandma is 108 years-old! About 80 years ago a gypsy told her that she would live to 112 years of age. She still mentions this now on each birthday she has, which shows how much of an influence this premonition has had over her life. We will have to see if she does make it to 112, but it's looking good so far. And I wonder if when she does get to 112, she will believe that is the end and give up, thus fulfilling the prophecy. Also, worth noting when I ask her what is the secret to living so long? She always replies with the same answer; 'hard boiled sweets.' So, you see saliva really is your friend as I mentioned in Anxiety Matters.

It's all about setting an intention and believing that it will come true 100%. It's why love and money spells work for so many people, because the intention is set in the subconscious so the mind will work to make that intention come true. It doesn't actually matter what you have to do in the spell, it's the belief in it working that makes it work. I could ask you to collect 50 white shoelaces and dance around them in your bedroom naked at night on a full moon, and it would have the exact same effect as any primal, tribalistic, ritualistic spell. If you have put effort into it, your mind then takes note and believes in the intention. Go and see a hypnotist. I don't mean a hypnotherapist. I'm talking about one that actually hypnotizes you. When I went to one, he utterly blew me away with how he was so easily able to hypnotize me without me even realising that he had. I presumed with my highly anxious mind that it would probably be really difficult if not impossible for him. He was showing off all the standard magic tricks of reading my mind and telling me what was written on the page I opened of the book before I even got it out my bag. I was like "No way, how are you doing this?" And he laughed and said "Ha, I hypnotised you in 5 minutes of you being here." I was like "No you really didn't, I'm not hypnotised in the slightest. I don't feel any different at all." So then he got me to go out into the hallway and look in the mirror and said "so how do you like your eyes?" When I looked at them my eyes were sparkling like glistening beautiful diamonds in the mirror. It was truly magical to see them like that, and it made me cry out with laughter. It was insane to me how he was able to control my subconscious, but also with how relaxed I was the whole way through it, in fact probably the most relaxed I've ever felt in my life. It concerns my paranoid sci-fi brain that hypnotism could be being used on us on a larger scale without us knowing, but let's not go there right now. There are so many other alternative things out there to try. Get out there and experience stuff you don't understand or that can't be explained by rational thinking.

Where are you now in your life? Where do you want to be in your life? Start opening your eyes and ears and listen out for that voice inside you that will tell you where to start, and then follow that flow. I promise it will be far more exciting than any movie you watch.

If you build it, they will come.....

Information Diet

More and more people are becoming self-aware now and are choosing to put themselves on 'information diets.' As we already know our brains are constantly downloading everything we see and hear, so we need to start narrowing the flood to stop us being overloaded with useless and harmful data. Have you ever noticed how you have nightmares when you have watched a horror film or a serial killer documentary? Have you noticed how unsettled you feel when you watch disturbing news stories? You may not even be consciously aware of it, there will just be something off in you and you won't be able to put your finger on it. The first thing you would get told if you want to unblock or unleash your creativity is to stop watching the news, period. Because the news is basically a brain washing control method to keep us all in line, to believe everyone is out to get us, so it's best to stick to what we know and not trust people. 'Divide and conquer.' Think what would happen if we all just got on really well? There would be a lot of stuff we would decide we wouldn't need and would get rid of it? The things we choose to give our attention to would change? The way we live would change? If you suffer with anxiety and depression the news is literally the worse thing you could watch, as it confirms all your negative thoughts that the world really is a frightening and depressing place. Trust me if you stop watching it you will be a lot happier in yourself. In the UK, news and politics are always hot topics and you're expected to know everything that is going on with them and also have an opinion about them. People I know have literally looked at me like I've just murdered someone when I say I don't know what they are on about when they start talking to me about a current horrendous news story. And I reply "well I was feeling pretty good until you told me that. Why did you tell me that? There is literally nothing I can do to help that person or situation is there? So now I just feel shitty." We have a saying here that 'no news is good news.'

Why is that? I always say I'd happily watch a 'good news' channel that only reports positive happy stories from around the globe. Think how great your day would start with listening to happy, fun and inspiring news first thing in the morning. This makes way more sense to me to make us all feel more harmonious and connected, but as I said before something like that would unite us too much. My mother is addicted to the television. She spends all day watching the 24-hour news channels and then all evening watching the soaps and dramas. The last time I visited her, when I left to go home she told me to make sure I didn't have my mobile phone on display on the way home as someone would attack me and steal it, and to be on the lookout for motorbikes with 2 people on them as the person on the back might throw acid in my face! *Lush!* Can you see how I was quite happy not even thinking about these things before this conversation? But she literally transmitted fear into my head, and no matter how much I tried to shake her comments off as ridiculous paranoia the thoughts and images were already there. It's no wonder my mother is so insecure in herself and life, she lives in permanent fear watching the news so much and then all those daft soaps in the evening which just have constant stress and drama in them. I sat and watched one with her as it was the only way I could spend time with her. And in just one half an hour episode some guy was having an affair with the woman over the road, someone murdered someone else, another character was being violently beaten up by their husband. And the disturbing thing about these soaps is that they are on a drip feed; one after the other, all bloody evening so you can't escape it if you're an addict. Why don't people realise this? They are called 'programs' for fuck sake! I'm not saying you have to give up tv completely, I enjoy tv viewing. I'm saying just lessen it and be more aware of what television is. Binge watching is talked about like it is a naughty but acceptable vice, but it's actually just as bad for you as binge drinking and binge eating. So, if you decide to go on an information diet too then just like any other diet you have to be disciplined with it. So set yourself targets of say one hour of tv a day and 30 mins of online time, and know before you go on either what you are going to be watching or looking at in that time, as that will save you wasted hours of pointless energy draining browsing. You'll actually enjoy it a lot more that way too, and you'll be choosier about how you spend that minimal set time. Now that I spend less time on social media I only read the posts I really want to, and I unfollow people that clog my newsfeed up with pointless ego driven fake filtered selfies or annoying boring self-important rants. We really do live in a world of instant gratification, where we expect everything instantly. We want to be stimulated and utterly blown away every time with what we view on tv. We ruthlessly flick through the options tutting and getting frustrated because we can't find anything spectacular, and then we realise we've spent all our evening just trying to find something that isn't even there and are totally pissed off with having wasted our evening.

Ask yourself why are you watching or viewing 'other peoples' creations so much? Wouldn't it be cool to spend time building your own creation? As I mentioned in the previous chapter your creation could be a product, service or a business, you can build 'anything' and it all starts in your mind. My all-time favourite film quote is 'If you build it they will come' it is from a film called Field of Dreams and it is about a guy living in the middle of nowhere in Iowa who hears a mysterious voice telling him 'if you build it they will come' whilst walking through his cornfield one night. So he builds a baseball field there which seems utter lunacy. Right at the end of the film they can see 100's of car lights heading towards them, thus fulfilling the prophecy of the voice 'if you build it, they will come.'

Speaking of other people's creations, are you aware of just how many you adhere to in your daily existence? Think about superstition, where did that come from? Do you know someone personally who walked under a ladder and then had something terrible happen to them straight away? No of course you don't. Or all this nonsense about 7 years bad luck for breaking a mirror. Or bad luck comes in 3's. Or Friday the 13th is unlucky. Or black cats are unlucky. There was always a high number of black cats in the animal shelter I worked in. I remember one day I went in and it was filled with only black cats. We have these superstitious beliefs installed in us at a young age from our predecessors, so we believe in them like they do without questioning why they believe in them or where they came from. When you do finally think about it, you realise how ridiculous it all is. I now purposely walk under any ladders I see. It's quite amusing watching other people's response to me strolling proudly underneath as they swerve out of the way. They will even put themselves in danger in the road just to avoid that ladder. Superstitions come from thousands of years ago. Why are you still honouring someone else's creation now? The same with Shakespeare. Yes, he was incredibly talented, but do you realise how much 'you' are channelling him? Here are just a few of Shakespeare's sayings; 'Heart of Gold. Good riddance. Wear your heart on your sleeve. Break the ice. What's done is done. Wild goose chase. Laughingstock. Green eyed monster. Love is blind. Makes your hair stand on end. Dead as a doornail. Eaten me out of house and home.' As I said that is just a few of his sayings. We just automatically repeat sayings that we have heard others use, we don't ever even question where it came from or what it actually means. I first became mindful of my words when I visited a Georgian mansion that had history dating back 500 years, and the tour guide proceeded to tell us where a large number of our sayings come from. Like 'daylight robbery' was from when they used to get taxed on how many windows they had, so a lot of the larger houses would brick up all windows apart from 6 of them, preventing them from receiving as much daylight, hence 'daylight robbery.' It amused me that I have said that saying myself a few times only understanding that it means to be taken advantage of financially. 'Pinch of salt' refers to older times when food was more easily swallowed with a small amount of salt. 'Saving face' refers to the 1500's where Queen Elizabeth made the white face and painted red lips on-trend. *still preferable to freaky clown eyebrows and trout pouts today.* And to stop the white paint sliding off their face in the evenings while they were sat socialising by the fire, they would have a reading shield in front of their face.

And we are not just haunted by older times, we are also possessed by many creations today. Did you know that for 100's of years engagement rings were gold and copper, not a diamond in sight? It was only from a hugely successful marketing campaign 'diamonds are forever' by a struggling Diamond company in 1947 that made diamonds a popular choice. By 1980 nearly all engagement rings were diamond rings. All because of that campaign. That is the power of marketing. That is the power of suggestive thought to the subconscious mind. That one company has successfully brainwashed you, as if you now try to think of an engagement ring you will instantly picture a diamond ring. There is another highly successful piece of jewellery I can think of; a charm bracelet that has been doing the rounds in the last few years. You think you pay enough for the bracelet, but they get you with the outrageously priced never-ending add on charms to put on it. Women are brainwashed to love them, because it's been so successfully marketed, and it has a domino effect; she's got it, so it must be good, so I want it too. And that is just 2 examples of successful marketing. We are bombarded all day every day with advertisements promoting other people's creations. Which is why it is so important to be mindful and step away as much as possible from the all-consuming consumerism that surrounds us.

There are other more sinister, yet seemingly harmless creations that have benefited from mass marketing. Coffee is one. Every second shop on the high street is now a coffee shop, each with a queue of at least 10 bleary eyed caffeine addicts all anxiously awaiting their next fix. Coffee is big business due to the explosion of the 'fancy coffee' in the last 10 years. Long gone is the bland gravelly instant sort we used to have to put up with throwing down our gobs. Now you can have it smooth and layered to your liking, with steamed milk and syrup flavourings, served up in posh tall glasses or soup bowl cups with pretty art designs on top which you can indulge and savour every sip slowly. When we arrange to meet up with friends it's always 'let's go for coffee.' I gave coffee up a few years ago because I had become too reliant on it and it was making my driving anxiety worse. But even now I feel pressure to say 'let's grab a coffee' as saying 'let's go for a tea or a juice' doesn't quite have the same ring to it. Cake is another one. Apparently cake makes everything better. Does it really? I don't really like cake, so I don't want to eat it, and the amount of times people have been so annoyed with me because I don't want to eat my body weight in cake with them to make them feel better about doing it. Wine is another big destructive socially acceptable habit hugely marketed mainly at women, and a lot of the time by other women. The whole 'it's wine o' clock somewhere in the world' premise with photos of women at their wits end reaching for their fishbowl glasses filled with 14% beneficial 'it will be alright now tonic' all over social media gives a green light to other women that this is what you do, and that it's allowed because every other woman is doing it, including celebrity women. I recently went looking for a birthday card for a girlfriend of mine who rarely drinks, and I struggled big time to find one that didn't mention either wine or gin. It's insidious the way alcohol marketing has led to alcoholism being portrayed as being playful and humorous. And that is what it is. Drinking every night is an addiction. And if drinking coffee every morning to wake you up and drinking wine every evening to calm you down is the only way you can function effectively through life then you do have a problem. I used alcohol nearly every day as a crutch for 20 years of my life because I didn't think I could cope with life without it. And I have so many friends that make comments and jokes about them being functioning alcoholics. They know they have a problem, but because it is so socially acceptable nowadays, they don't have to feel bad or do anything about it. In fact it's so acceptable now that it's actually expected of you to drink alcohol, and frowned upon if you don't, and you are made to feel you are somehow letting the side down if you refuse a drink. I have had many arguments with friends in the last couple of years because I have cut back on drinking to the point that sometimes I don't fancy a drink for months. They will push a glass of wine into my hand saying "you know you want to" and when I reply "no actually I don't want to tonight" they take it extremely personally that I am purposely trying to ruin their night, and that we will not be able to connect and talk to each other in the same way with one of us sober as both of us drinking. The honest truth is that me not having to drink alcohol highlights them having to drink alcohol.

Start waking up and questioning everything, and that means even the closest people around you. Start choosing what you are going to put in your own information diet. I choose to spend a lot of my free time reading and writing. I usually have 3 or 4 books on the go at once. *4 books? you said you were on an information diet genius!* I like being able to flick between genres, and I always have at least 2 non-fiction books, whether that's a self-help book, an autobiography or something else. I love a twisty thriller but again I try to stay away from anything too violently graphic like characters being tortured or buried alive. Torture porn is very lazy writing, and you deserve better than that with your investment in a story. I like easy going thrillers, so I tend to enjoy stuff like Harlan Coben as they are quite simple but very clever and twisty, and I love the humour he puts into his stories. It feels like he's really trying to connect with the reader rather than just telling a well thought out story. The other benefit from reading more than one book at the same time is that I'm not just concentrating on one person's creation, and usually you will create a few synchronicities when you are reading a few stories together, which then becomes your creation of it. There are so many other activities to do that can really benefit your mind, such as watching motivational videos and inspirational movies. Listening to audiobooks (they are free on YouTube) they are so good for focus and really relaxing. Give your brain a workout by playing brain games. Start writing something, it could even be a diary or journal to help connect to yourself. Go for beach or countryside walks, there is so much personal space on a beach or out in the country, it's almost like having the entire world to yourself. And being in nature is so beneficial, the natural sounds, the raw breath-taking beauty. Have you ever been to the beach late at night and listen to how loud the waves crashing in are? Don't let anyone put you down for enjoying these types of activities. It's the same as the drinking alcohol, people won't like you highlighting their lack of self-care, and some people just won't get it and will just want you to sit in a pub with them all afternoon or trail around the shops with them buying more clothes that you don't need. Connect with your inner child as much as possible. When we are connected to our child selves is when we are most authentic and connected to source, because we don't have the barriers of self-criticism and rational thinking. I see it with my 5-year-old stepson, who just wildly throws paint around on a picture and has absolutely no care in what it looks like or if the colours match. I once bought him a dinosaur painting kit and I was quite excited about painting them in their natural colours described on the box, but my stepson said "I want to paint one blue with red spots and the other one orange with green stripes" and that was it. No rhyme nor reason to it, he just felt like doing it that way. So that's what we did.

Start tapping into your own creations. What are your talents? What do you enjoy doing? What do 'you' feel you are good at (forgetting other people's opinions or criticisms)?

Remember 'you are what you absorb'.

Balancing Act

Life is one big fat long balancing act. Especially nowadays when you are expected to spin multiple plates all at once; family, partner, friends, career, hobbies. The trouble is at some points we will drop some plates, this isn't something we can avoid. We cannot expect for things to go right for us 247, that is not how life is. There is balance in every area in life. Where there is dark there is light. Where there is success there is failure. Where there is good there is bad. Think about online review sites you look at; you will get great reviews and truly terrible reviews for the exact same product or place. Social media is massively negative in so many ways as it makes it easier for people to get away with behaving badly, and it isolates and depresses people as they feel inadequate and can make life seem completely superficial. But at the exact same time social media is amazingly positive. It unites people and brings them together on a huge scale that would never have been possible before the internet. When there is a crisis or a disaster people will arrange gatherings so people can turn up to a location to help, or they start crowdfunding appeals so people can contribute with money to help. Social media also reunites distant relatives and long-lost friends too. Volunteering at the animal shelter showed me the very best in people, and also the very worst. I could not believe that a human being could treat an animal in such a terrible way. It was truly sickening and made me ashamed to be a human. But on the flip side there were animals there I thought would never get taken home (a term they use when a pet gets a new loving home) because they were really old with expensive long term health problems which you would think would put people off but it didn't, those pets always got taken home, and the turnaround there was fast. That really restored my faith in humans that they are pretty amazing really. Another example is the numerous therapists I went to over the years, some were good, a lot were absolute shit. I remember one that used to sit in front of me continuously looking at the clock behind me that was positioned directly above my head to see how long left she had with me, and she didn't even try to hide the look of boredom on her face. That's another good reason to question everything, as just because someone is qualified in a job does not mean they are actually any good at it.

You might think you would love to be able to eat out at fancy restaurants every night, but the reality is you'd get bored of it quite quickly and probably overweight quite quickly too. When I go away on holiday by the fourth night of eating out, I'm fed up with it, and I just want some good old-fashioned beans on toast. The same way as I love spending time on my own writing, reading, watching films, pottering about. But if I did this every single day, I would get seriously depressed and anxious. I need other people in my life to give me variety and diversity.

Don't restrict yourself with one way of doing things either. I love hard rock music, but I equally love hard dance music, they are classed as opposites, but they are actually remarkably similar. I enjoy fine dining, but I equally enjoy simple foods. I like going to loud wild parties, but I also enjoy sitting on my own silently in nature. They say variety is the spice of life. Variety can definitely help creativity to flow, as there are no restrictions on it. It is said that the definition of insanity is doing the same thing over and over again. So switch things up. If you are a writer and you are struggling to motivate yourself then get a buddy writer online where you can write things together, completely separate from your own writing work. Just doing this will motivate you to write your own stuff. Have a wide variety of friends in your life with different mindsets who will expand your thinking, as you will get varied opinions from them. When you are getting help or advice from a professional don't just go for the first easy option, explore who/what else is out there. Just because someone tells you they are an expert at something or have a certificate or qualification does not mean they know all there is to know about that subject or are any good at it. Take your time and look around and go with who or what feels right to you.

Please the different parts of your brain. Don't let it go stale by giving it the same regurgitated stuff over and over, it deserves better from you. You deserve better.

Does your life have balance at the moment? Make a plan of how you can make time for all areas of leading a happy life; work, friends, hobbies, relaxation.

So, start looking forward to the rest of your life from this moment, and remember without goals, dreams will always just be dreams.

Taking The P's Out Of You

My last chapter guys *sniff sniff* is all about the 4 deadly p's that are capable of destroying us and our dreams on a daily basis if we let them. So we need to be aware of them and kick ass them into touch.

Procrastination

I am the Procrastination Princess! I don't care who you are or how much you say you procrastinate; it will never be as much as me! I would seriously win Olympic medals in it if it was a sport. It's one of my faults that I openly admit to and am still working hard to overcome. When I have a task to do that my brain deems as hard, challenging, boring or taxing, it will instantly go into avoidance mode. Which usually involves making cups of tea, researching stuff online which links to other research online which has nothing to do with what I began with, and then I'll start reading blogs about that research and start reading all the opinions of other people on that blog at the comments section on that blog. Basically, I just find other things to do to avoid what I know I should be doing. Anything to use up my time so I haven't got time to do the task I am supposed to be doing. Something gets triggered in my brain that tells me 'this is going to be hard or boring with no reward, so let's just avoid it completely'. The fact of the matter is there is a reward for completing the task. Once you've done it you feel really good and accomplished about having done it and having one more job ticked off the list, and it stops that lingering nagging feeling in the background that you have stuff to do. So the best thing really is to just sit down and do it because it's not going to go away, and every time you take charge and 'just do it' that is a smash in the face of a major killer P!

Perception

We do not see things how they are; we see them how we are. This is a gamechanger when you have this realisation about life. My sister and I had exactly the same upbringing but have a completely different experience to it. We are like chalk and cheese as people so it's obvious our perception on things would be like chalk and cheese too. It doesn't make one of us right and one of us wrong, because it's about our own perception. And you will never be able to change someone else's perception, as you cannot be in their head to know how theirs works. This is why people pleasing is such a huge waste of time, as they will never perceive you in the exact same way as you want them to.

Presumption

I used to always expect the worst. This came from growing up in a family who expected bad luck. One of my mother's favourite lines was 'winning the lottery wouldn't happen to us' even though she plays it every week. I was taught to presume the worst of every situation. But, when bad things happen to us, are they really that bad? Most of the time we can sort them out and move on from them, and even if they are bad, we can learn a lot from them. Don't presume to know everything or presume to know how things will turn out, or presume to know what someone else is thinking, you cannot possibly know these things, so don't waste your precious time on them. And stop trying to guess the outcome of everything, and just accept what is meant to happen for you will happen for you. And you are going to learn from all of your experiences, good and bad, and they will add to your incredible unique story.

Perfectionism

This is probably the biggest P taker. Perfectionism is the slayer of dreams. It can annihilate your goals before you even start them. I used to have terrible OCD based around perfectionism. There were even days when I wouldn't go to work because a couple of things had gone wrong for me in the morning like the toaster deciding to stop working, or not being able to find the shoes I wanted to wear that day. I would take that as a personal message from the universe to stay at home and wait for reset the next morning. It held me back in so many experiences in my life, as if something wasn't just right or the way I had envisioned it then I didn't want to know. Fortunately, I've learnt over time to accept and even embrace imperfection in my life. I see it now as an enjoyable challenge. If I really want to do something, I now just see my goal at the end of a fun obstacle course. It's all part of the journey and a chance to show off your strength to yourself. Recently I wanted to take up running again after many years, and I decided to start the next day, but the next day was suddenly filled with thunderstorms and soaked grass. Now the old me would have taken that as a sign to not take up running and to just forget about it. But instead I thought 'no I wanted to start running today and that is what I am going to do!' Yes I wasn't able to get as good results as I would have had had it been dry, and yes I got absolutely soaked, and yes I got some very strange looks, but I still achieved my goal of running that day. It certainly wasn't perfect or pretty but I did it.

Start believing in yourself and start trusting in your decisions. 'I made a decision based on the information I had at the time.' Do your best. It's more than good enough. Stop striving for perfection. Things don't have to be a snug fit. Never ever take 'life' personally. Shit happens. And get used to the fact that life is unfair. We can't control what happens around us, but we can control how we are as people and how we react to situations.

There is a saying 'you don't know someone until you live with them' it is so true. I got to know the real John and Laura from living with them. Had I not lived with them I wouldn't have seen their faults and flaws, and would never have realised that behind closed doors people that appear perfect from the outside are anything but perfect, and I wouldn't have wanted them to be any other way. And I know now if I moved in with The Murrays, I would see all their faults and flaws too. Because we all have them. None of us are perfect.

I know this book will be far from perfect for some people. But this is the way it came out, and I wrote it from my heart and soul so it's good enough for me. HNB read over it for me and said, "Yeah I like it, but you can't write numbers as numbers in a book, you have to write them as words." I replied; "Why?" And he replied, "Because that's the right way of doing it." I thought of my 5-year-old stepson and the dinosaurs and smiled and simply said "Well I like it this way."

So, as I said in the beginning, I guess I wrote this to make all my many years of suffering worth it, and that they actually had a purpose. As I couldn't have written this for you otherwise. And I truly hope it does help you in some way, even if only to make you realise you are not alone. I have also just realised as I write this, I've also written it for 5-year-old Tara Jean, alone in the Wendy house, isolated for the first of many times in her life. Maybe that is why she is looking into space and smiling, maybe she already knows I've written this.

So please do feel free to email me at sparkstara@aol.com if you would like to share your thoughts, or leave me a review on Amazon (smiley face with heart-shaped eyes) which would be **hugely** appreciated *as long as it's nice.*

Disclaimer: My book is simply for information and entertainment purposes. I am not a medical practitioner or a nutritionist. This book is not to be perceived as professional advice in regard to health. Please always check with your doctor before following any advice or information given in this book.

Love and light to you x

Printed in Great Britain
by Amazon

57819798R00081